Grade 2

Addison-Wesley Mathematics

Challenges Workbook

▲ Addison-Wesley Publishing Company

Menlo Park, California ▪ *Reading, Massachusetts* ▪ *New York*
Don Mills, Ontario ▪ *Wokingham, England* ▪ *Amsterdam* ▪ *Bonn*
Sydney ▪ *Singapore* ▪ *Tokyo* ▪ *Madrid* ▪ *San Juan*

Copyright © by Addison-Wesley Publishing Company, Inc.
The workbook pages in this publication are designed to be used with
appropriate duplicating equipment to reproduce copies for classroom
use. Addison-Wesley Publishing Company grants permission to
classroom teachers to reproduce these pages. Printed in the United
States of America. Published simultaneously in Canada.

ISBN 0-201-27211-3

ABCDEFGHIJK-HC-943210

D1126867

Table of Contents

Space Math

Draw the space creature. Use mental math.

1. The space creature has 1 less than 2 heads.

2. It has 2 more than 1 eye.

3. It has 5 less than 6 noses.

4. It has 2 more than 4 arms.

5. It has 6 more than 2 ears.

6. It has 9 less than 11 smiling mouths.

7. It has 8 less than 14 legs.

8. It has 3 more than 4 tails.

Addition Riddles

Complete the addition sentences in the box.

3 + 1 = ____ riddles	2 + 3 = ____ is
6 + 2 = ____ I	1 + 2 = ____ adding
1 + 1 = ____ doing	2 + 4 = ____ like
5 + 2 = ____ fun	

Look at the words next to your answers.
Each word matches a number.
Write these words under the numbers below.
What do the addition riddles say? Read them to a friend.

8	6	2	4

_____ .

3	5	7	

_____ .

8	6	3	

_____ .

2	4	5	7

_____ .

Use with text pages 3 – 4.

Name _____

Three in a Row

> Dear Family,
>   We have just completed a lesson on subtraction facts. As you play this game with your child, say the subtraction sentences aloud.

Take turns subtracting.
Find three 3s in a row to win.
Draw a line.

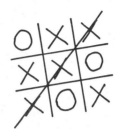

$8 - 5 =$	$7 - 2 =$	$4 - 2 =$
$5 - 4 =$	$6 - 3 =$	$8 - 7 =$
$7 - 3 =$	$8 - 2 =$	$5 - 2 =$

Play again.
Find three differences in a row that are the same
to win. Draw a line.

$6 - 3 =$	$4 - 3 =$	$8 - 3 =$
$7 - 4 =$	$7 - 2 =$	$8 - 6 =$
$6 - 1 =$	$8 - 6 =$	$6 - 4 =$

Name _____

My Birthday

Look at a calendar. Finish these sentences.

1. My birthday is _____ _____.
   (month)   (number)

2. My birthday is on the _____
   day of the month.   (ordinal number)

3. Right now, I am _____ years old.
                   (number)

4. This year, my birthday is on a _____.
                                  (day of the week)

5. I will be _____ years old.
             (number)

6. On the Sunday after my birthday, I will be
   _____ years and _____ days old.
   (number)   (number)

7. There are _____ days in the month
             (number)
   before my birthday.

8. There are _____ days in the month
             (number)
   after my birthday.

Color Cube Patterns

Play this game with a partner. Take turns.
Use 16 cubes of 4 colors. Arrange them in a 4-by-4 square.
Cubes of the same color
should not touch each other.
If you choose red, blue, white,
and yellow, your square
might look like this.

R	B	R	B
Y	W	Y	W
R	B	R	B
Y	W	Y	W

Ask your partner to look away.

1. Remove 1 cube from a
corner of the square.
Ask your partner to tell what color is missing.
Take away 2 or 3 cubes.
Can your partner put them back in the right place?

2. Snap 2 side-by-side cubes together.
Take them both away. Turn them around.
Put them back.
Can your partner find the turned-around
cubes and turn them back?
Try this with 4 cubes snapped together.

3. Think up your own color cube game.
Try using 36 cubes of 4 colors in a 6-by-6 square.

Name _____

Bingo!

Work with a friend to make 16 cards for this game.
Write one subtraction fact on each card:

$6-3=3$ $7-3=4$ $6-1=5$ $6-2=4$

$7-5=2$ $7-1=6$ $6-0=6$ $5-4=1$

$8-8=0$ $8-1=7$ $5-2=3$ $5-5=0$

$8-6=2$ $8-3=5$ $8-4=4$ $4-2=2$

Complete the addition facts on the game board below.

You need 2 players, counters, the game cards you made.
Mix up the cards and put them facedown.
Pick a card. Find the matching addition fact.
Cover the addition fact with a counter.
Play until someone has four in a row.

$3+3=$ ___	$4+3=$ ___	$5+1=$ ___	$4+2=$ ___
$5+2=$ ___	$6+1=$ ___	$6+0=$ ___	$1+4=$ ___
$8+0=$ ___	$7+1=$ ___	$3+2=$ ___	$0+5=$ ___
$2+6=$ ___	$5+3=$ ___	$4+4=$ ___	$2+2=$ ___

Name _____

Look! Up in the Sky!

Write the answers in the circles.
Put your pencil on the words "Start here."
Draw a line between the related subtraction facts.

$$\begin{array}{r} 8 \\ -7 \\ \hline \end{array}$$ ◯ ← Start here.

$$\begin{array}{r} 8 \\ -5 \\ \hline \end{array}$$ ◯

$$\begin{array}{r} 8 \\ -3 \\ \hline \end{array}$$ ◯

$$\begin{array}{r} 8 \\ -1 \\ \hline \end{array}$$ ◯

$$\begin{array}{r} 7 \\ -3 \\ \hline \end{array}$$ ◯

$$\begin{array}{r} 8 \\ -6 \\ \hline \end{array}$$ ◯

$$\begin{array}{r} 7 \\ -4 \\ \hline \end{array}$$ ◯

$$\begin{array}{r} 7 \\ -5 \\ \hline \end{array}$$ ◯

$$\begin{array}{r} 8 \\ -2 \\ \hline \end{array}$$ ◯

$$\begin{array}{r} 7 \\ -2 \\ \hline \end{array}$$ ◯

What did you find in the sky? _____

Addison-Wesley | All Rights Reserved

CS-2 Use with text pages 13–14. **7**

Name _____

Amazing Fact Families

Complete the fact families in the six boxes below.
Then trace the path from one part of each fact
family to the other part. Use a different color
crayon to connect each fact family.

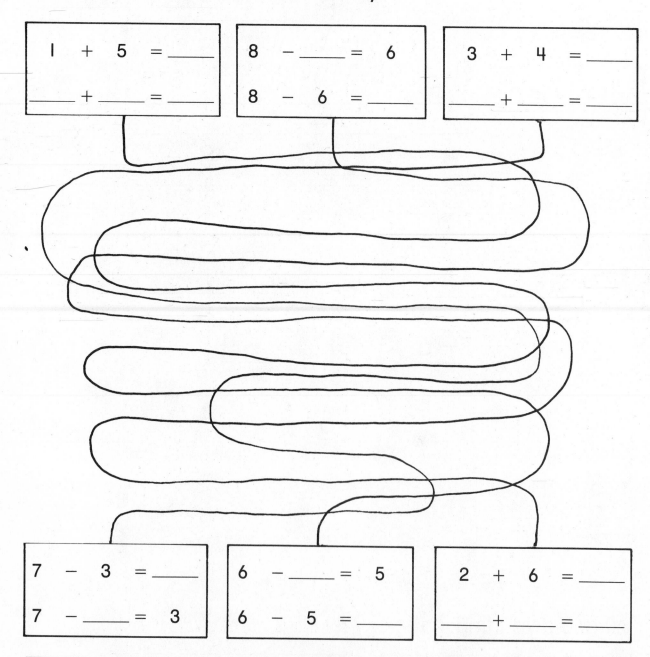

1 + 5 = ____	
____ + ____ = ____	

8 − ____ = 6	
8 − 6 = ____	

3 + 4 = ____	
____ + ____ = ____	

7 − 3 = ____	
7 − ____ = 3	

6 − ____ = 5	
6 − 5 = ____	

2 + 6 = ____	
____ + ____ = ____	

Use with text pages 15 – 16.

Playground Problems

Finish the picture below.
Draw some boys and girls on the swings and seesaws.
Then finish the number sentences so they describe
the picture.

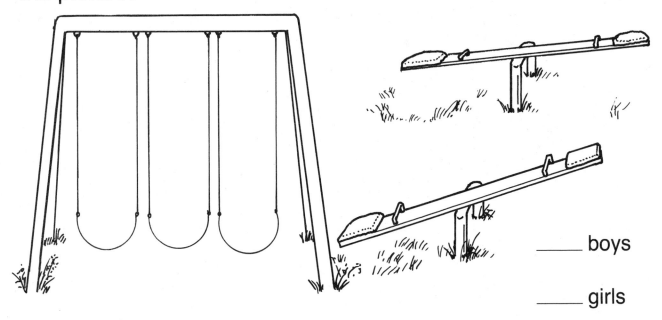

_____ boys

_____ girls

_____ boys _____ girls

1. _____ + _____ = _____ boys and girls on swings.

2. _____ – _____ = _____ more _____ than _____
on the swings.

3. _____ + _____ = _____ boys and girls on seesaws.

4. _____ – _____ = _____ more _____ than _____
on the seesaws.

Math Bingo

Dear Family Member:
    Your child has just learned about counting on to add 1, 2, and 3 to a number, and about how to add zero. Play this game with your child to reinforce these addition facts.

Play with a family member. Each player chooses a game board. Toss a bean or a paper clip on the answer board. Color an expression on your game board that has that sum. Say **Bingo** when all your squares are colored.

Answer Board

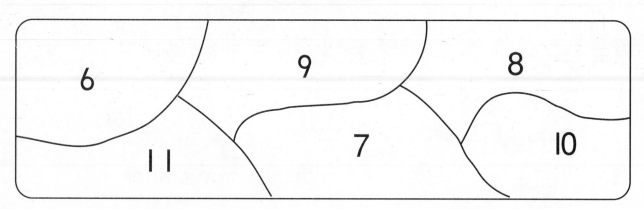

| 6 | | 9 | | 8 |
| 11 | | | 7 | | 10 |

Game Board

6 + 0	1 + 8	8 + 3
9 + 2	2 + 6	0 + 7
5 + 3	2 + 8	7 + 3
7 + 1	0 + 9	1 + 6

Game Board

2 + 4	9 + 1	3 + 5
5 + 1	6 + 3	1 + 10
0 + 8	1 + 8	2 + 9
5 + 2	7 + 0	3 + 8

Name _____

Crazy Caterpillar

You need: one or more friends,
a spinner with numbers 4 to 9,
a marker for each player.

Rules: Put the markers on **Start**.
Spin the spinner.
Double the number on the spinner.
Move your marker that number of spaces
on the caterpillar.
Now it is your friend's turn.
The first one to get to the leaf wins.

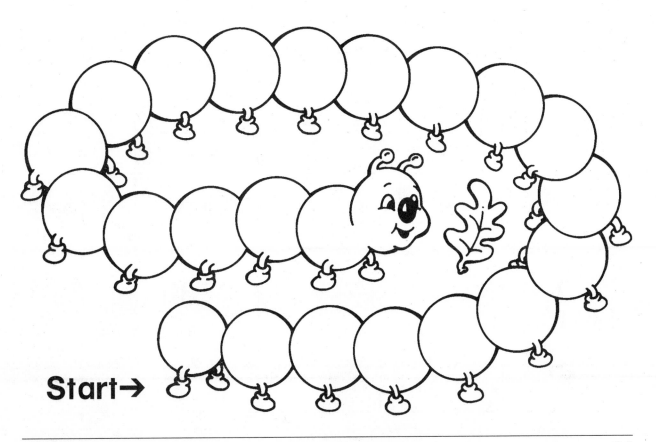

Start →

Name _____

Doubles-Plus-Ones Game

You need: one or more friends,
a spinner with numbers I to 8,
lots of markers.

Rules: Spin the spinner.
Double the number and add I.
Cover a number that matches the sum.
Now it is your friend's turn.
The first one to get 5 markers in a row
wins.

17	5	13	9	13
9	3	15	I I	7
7	I I	13	17	15
3	5	9	13	3
15	17	I I	7	5

Name _____

What Is the Question?

Make your own addition problems that have the given answers.

1.

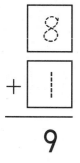

$$\begin{array}{r} 8 \\ + 1 \\ \hline 9 \end{array}$$

$$\begin{array}{r} \square \\ + \square \\ \hline 9 \end{array}$$

$$\begin{array}{r} \square \\ + \square \\ \hline 9 \end{array}$$

$$\begin{array}{r} \square \\ + \square \\ \hline 9 \end{array}$$

$$\begin{array}{r} \square \\ + \square \\ \hline 9 \end{array}$$

2.

$$\begin{array}{r} \square \\ + \square \\ \hline 10 \end{array}$$

$$\begin{array}{r} \square \\ + \square \\ \hline 10 \end{array}$$

$$\begin{array}{r} \square \\ + \square \\ \hline 10 \end{array}$$

$$\begin{array}{r} \square \\ + \square \\ \hline 10 \end{array}$$

$$\begin{array}{r} \square \\ + \square \\ \hline 10 \end{array}$$

3.

$$\begin{array}{r} \square \\ + \square \\ \hline 11 \end{array}$$

$$\begin{array}{r} \square \\ + \square \\ \hline 11 \end{array}$$

$$\begin{array}{r} \square \\ + \square \\ \hline 11 \end{array}$$

$$\begin{array}{r} \square \\ + \square \\ \hline 11 \end{array}$$

$$\begin{array}{r} \square \\ + \square \\ \hline 11 \end{array}$$

Name _____

Birthday Survey

Take a survey. Find out the birthday of each classmate. Tally the birthdays by month.

January	February	March	April

May	June	July	August

September	October	November	December

Which month has the most birthdays?_____

Which month has the fewest birthdays? _____
How many students have their birthday in the same

month as you do?_____
Share the data with your classmates.

Target Ten

Play with a friend.

Player I puts a marker on a number.

Player 2 puts a marker on the number needed to make 10.

5	9	6	I
3	7	8	10
0	2	4	5

Play again.

This time player 2 goes first.

Play until you cover all the numbers.

Now try **Target Twelve**.

4	0	3	6	10
5	I	8	7	6
6	9	II	12	2

Spin to Add

Use your spinner.
Add 9 to the number
you spin.
Keep your score on the
scorecard below.
Put a √ for each sum.

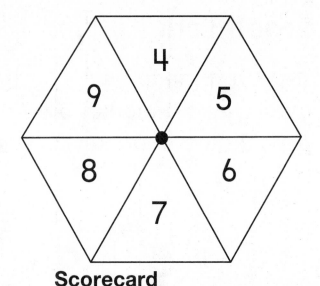

Scorecard

Sums of	13	14	15	16	17	18

1. Write numbers on this spinner so that when you add 9, you can make only sums of 13, 15, and 17.

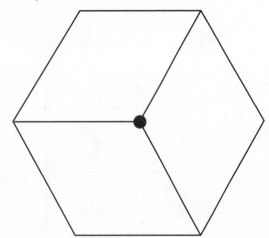

2. Write numbers on this spinner so that when you add 9, you can make only sums of 14, 16, and 18.

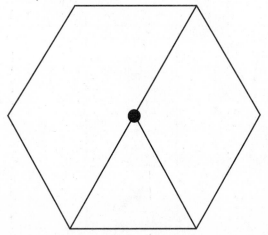

Name _____

Try This Make Ten Machine!

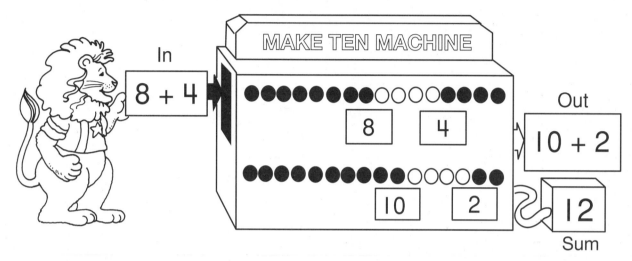

Complete the out cards. Then find the sums.

	In	Out	Sum
1.	8 + 6	10 + 4	14

	In	Out	Sum
2.	4 + 9	10 + ___	

3.	7 + 4	10 + ___	

4.	7 + 5	10 + ___	

5.	6 + 8	10 + ___	

6.	9 + 5	10 + ___	

7.	5 + 8	10 + ___	

8.	8 + 5	10 + ___	

9.	6 + 7	10 + ___	

10.	5 + 9	10 + ___	

Name _____

The Road to 18

Follow the rules.
Find the road to 18.

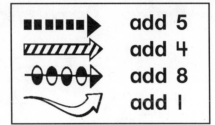

1.

2.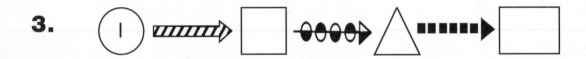

3.

4.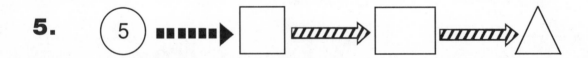

5.

Make your own.

6.

Name _____

Across and Down

Each ⊞ has the same sum when you add across and down. Write the missing numbers.
Make some of your own.
Use a calculator to help you.

1.

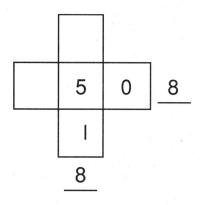

2.

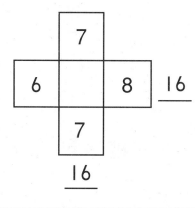

3.

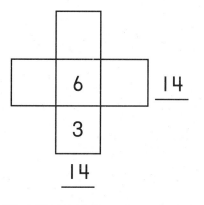

4.

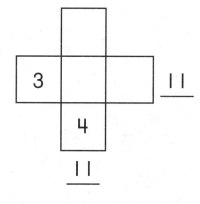

5.

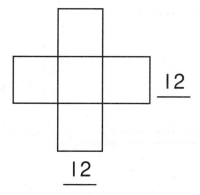

6.

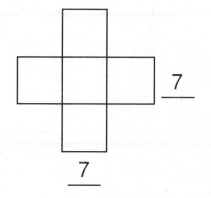

Critical Thinking

2-11

Name _____

What Is for Lunch?

Pick I sandwich and I drink.
Write 9 different lunches you can have.

1. _____ and _____

2. _____ and _____

3. _____ and _____

4. _____ and _____

5. _____ and _____

6. _____ and _____

7. _____ and _____

8. _____ and _____

9. _____ and _____

20   Use with text pages 43-44.   **CS-2**

Addison-Wesley | All Rights Reserved

Name _____

Turtle Race

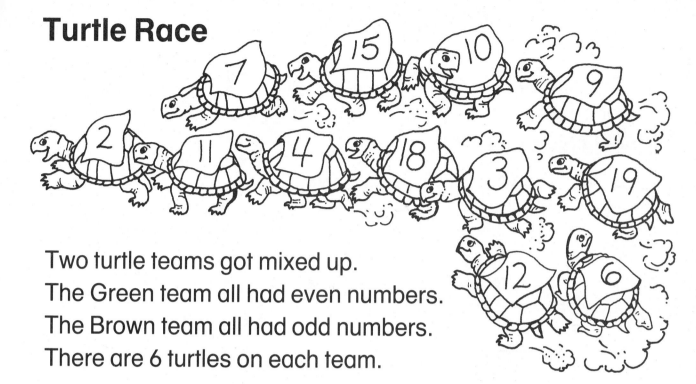

Two turtle teams got mixed up.
The Green team all had even numbers.
The Brown team all had odd numbers.
There are 6 turtles on each team.

1. Write the numbers for the turtles on the Green team.

2. Write the numbers for the turtles on the Brown team.

3. Two more turtles join the Green team.
Give them numbers. Do not use the number of a
turtle above.

Make Your Own Pattern

Work with a partner.

Color squares to show a growing pattern.

Decide on a rule. Take turns.

Use one of these rules or make up your own.

- Color 1 more each time.
- Color 4 more each time.
- Color 2 more, then 3 more, then 4 more. . . .

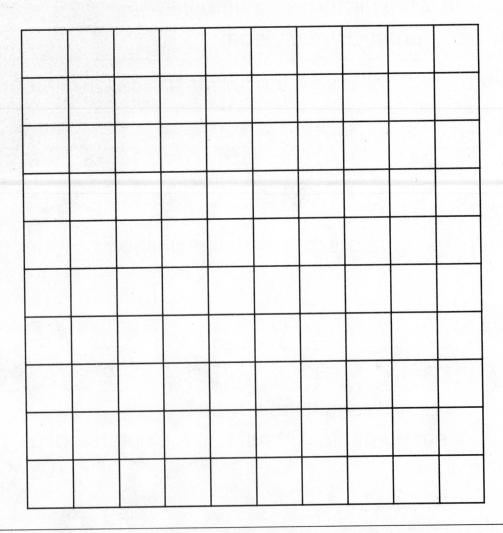

Follow the Pattern

Color the circles to make a pattern.
Start in the middle. Use two or three colors.
Read your pattern to a friend.

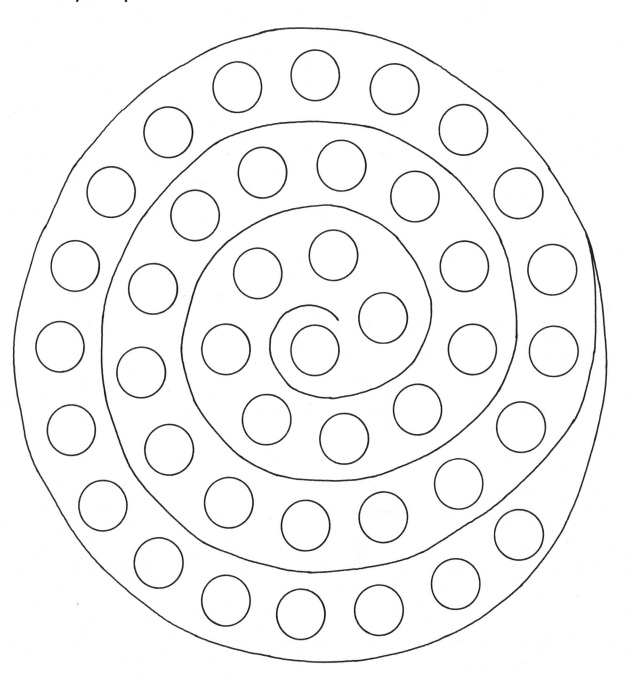

Name _____

Pattern Talk

Work with a partner.

1. Color the small squares to make a pattern.
Use two or three colors.

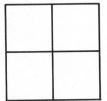 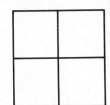 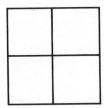 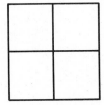

Ask your partner to tell what pattern you made.

---

2. Have your partner color the small triangles to make
a pattern. Use two or three colors.

  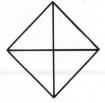 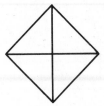

Tell what pattern your partner made.

---

3. This time color the small squares to start a pattern.
Leave the last figure blank.

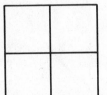 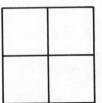 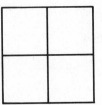 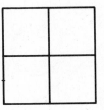

Ask your partner to finish the pattern.

Use with text pages 55–56.

A Time to Vote

Color the graph to show the votes.

Votes for School President

Joan ﬀﬀ ﬀﬀ ﬀﬀ ﬀﬀ ﬀﬀ ﬀﬀ
Bill ﬀﬀ ﬀﬀ ﬀﬀ ﬀﬀ ﬀﬀ ﬀﬀ ﬀﬀ
Jack ﬀﬀ ﬀﬀ ﬀﬀ
Ann ﬀﬀ ﬀﬀ ﬀﬀ ﬀﬀ ﬀﬀ
Sue ﬀﬀ ﬀﬀ ﬀﬀ ﬀﬀ ﬀﬀ ﬀﬀ ﬀﬀ ﬀﬀ ﬀﬀ
Fred ﬀﬀ ﬀﬀ ﬀﬀ ﬀﬀ ﬀﬀ ﬀﬀ ﬀﬀ

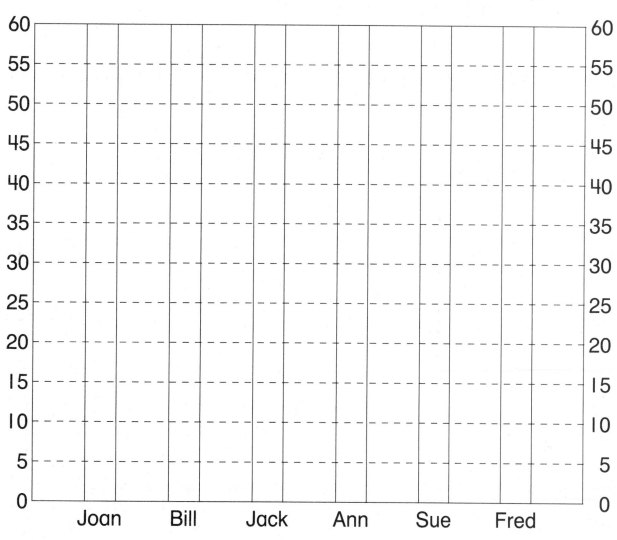

Votes for School President

Graph the Sums

Play with a partner.
You will need 2 cubes numbered 1 to 6.
Roll the cubes and name the sum.
Color a space next to that sum.
Take turns. Stop when one column is full.

2						
3						
4						
5						
6						
7						
8						
9						
10						
11						
12						

Which sum is rolled most often? _____ Least often? _____

Play again. Compare your two graphs.

Sea Shells

5 children made a tally of the shells they found.

Shells Found

Ben	⳾卌 卌 卌 卌
Sara	卌 卌 卌 卌 卌 卌
Dan	卌 卌 卌
Patty	卌 卌 卌 卌 卌 卌 卌
Rita	卌 卌 卌 卌 卌

Finish the pictograph to show the data.

Each equals 5 shells.

Shells Found

Ben	🐚 🐚 🐚 🐚
Sara	
Dan	
Patty	
Rita	

Share your graph with a partner.
Ask each other questions about the graph.

Name _____

At the Zoo

At the Children's Zoo you can
feed the llama for 5¢. Fill in the table.
Look for a pattern.

Cups of food	1	2	3				
cost	5¢	10¢	15¢				

Use the table to answer the questions.

1. Emily has 25¢. How many times can she feed

the llama? _____

2. Two children have 10¢ each. How many times can

they feed the llama? _____

3. How many times could you feed the llama with 30¢?

_____

4. Matthew has 37¢. He feeds the llama 7 times.

How much money does he have left? _____

Think about the pattern.

5. How many times could you feed the llama with 50¢?

_____

Name _____

Climb Down the Ladder

You need: a friend, a spinner with numbers 0 to 5,
and 12 paper clips for each player.

Rules: Each player puts 1 paper clip on each step of the ladder.
Take turns. Spin.

12
11
10
9
8
7
6
5
4
3
2
1

Subtract the number
on the spinner from
the number on the ladder.
Start on step ‖ 12 ‖.
Remove the number of
clips that matches the
number on the spinner.

If you cannot subtract
the number on the spinner
from the number on the step,
you lose your turn. The
first player who lands
exactly on step ‖ 1 ‖ wins.

12
11
10
9
8
7
6
5
4
3
2
1

Name _____

Subtraction Riddles

Complete the subtraction sentences in the box.
Look at the words next to your answers.
Each word matches a number.
Write these words under the numbers below.
What does the subtraction riddle say?
Read it to a friend.

$6 - 3 =$ ____ your	$10 - 5 =$ ____ What is
$16 - 8 =$ ____ Ginger	$4 - 2 =$ ____ name
$12 - 6 =$ ____ bite	$2 - 1 =$ ____ No
$8 - 4 =$ ____ Does	$18 - 9 =$ ____ snaps
$14 - 7 =$ ____ dog's	

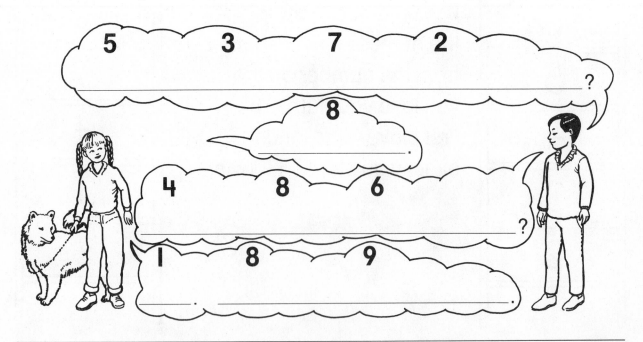

Name _____

Juggle the Numbers

Put each number in the correct place.
Use no other numbers.

10
$-\bigcirc$
___
$\bigcirc$

9
$-\bigcirc$
___
$\bigcirc$

9
$-\bigcirc$
___
$\bigcirc$

10
$-\bigcirc$
___
$\bigcirc$

10
$-\bigcirc$
___
$\bigcirc$

Name _____

Leapfrog

This is a game to play by yourself.

You need: a penny, a counter, and a pencil.

Rules: Put the counter on the middle frog.
Toss the penny.
If it lands **heads** up, make a tally mark under
HEADS and move the counter one frog to the left.
If it lands **tails** up, make a tally mark under
TAILS and move the counter one frog to the right.
Play until you reach one side or the other.
Predict whether you will toss heads or tails more often,
or about the same number for each. Play 3 times.
Total the tallies. Was your prediction close?

	HEADS move left	Total	TAILS move right	Total
Game 1				
Game 2				
Game 3				

Heads ←   Tails →

It's a Fact

Write your own subtraction fact for each difference.

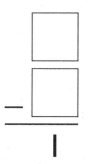

1

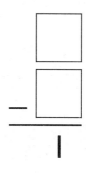

2

1

3

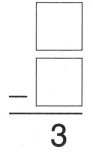

3

2

2

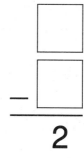

1

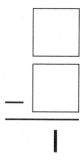

2

3

1

3

Subtraction Toss

START	3	0	8	5	1	7	4	2	6

FINISH		0

You need: 1 more friends, 1 penny, and 1 marker for each player.

Rules: Put your marker on **START**.
Toss a penny.
If it lands on heads, move 1 space.
If it lands on tails, move 2 spaces.
Read the number on the space.
Make up a subtraction fact with that number as the difference.
Take turns.
The first person to get to **FINISH** wins.

Left column (top to bottom): 5, 3, 1, 7, 4, 2, 6

Right column (top to bottom): 0, 8, 2, 3, 5, 1, 7, 4

Bottom row: 8, 4, 7, 1, 5, 2, 3, 0, 6

Use with text pages 79–80.

Name _____

Doubles Bingo

You need: 1 friend, 2 number cubes, and 2 different-color crayons.
Rules: Choose a crayon. Color the FREE space on the game board.
Take turns tossing the cubes.
Use the numbers on the top of the cubes
to write a subtraction fact.

$$3 - 2 = 1$$
$$3 - 1 = 2$$

Find the related subtraction fact on the
game board and color that space.
If the space has been colored, you lose your turn.
If you roll $6 - 3$, $4 - 2$, or $2 - 1$, color a **Doubles** space.
The first player to color 5 spaces in a row wins.

$5 - 0 = 5$	$3 - 2 = 1$	$2 - 0 = 2$	**Doubles**	$4 - 0 = 4$
Doubles	$4 - 3 = 1$	$6 - 2 = 4$	$6 - 5 = 1$	$3 - 0 = 3$
$5 - 1 = 4$	$1 - 0 = 1$	**FREE**	$5 - 4 = 1$	**Doubles**
$5 - 3 = 2$	**Doubles**	$3 - 1 = 2$	$6 - 4 = 2$	$6 - 0 = 6$
Doubles	$6 - 1 = 5$	$4 - 1 = 3$	$5 - 2 = 3$	**Doubles**

House Numbers

Work with a partner. Pick a number.
Write it on the door of the house.
In one part of the top window, write an addition sentence
with the number as the sum.
In one part of the bottom window, have your partner write
a sentence with different addends to make the same sum.
Finish each other's fact family by writing number
sentences in the other parts of each window.
Take turns. Play again. Use your partner's sheet.
Pick a different number.

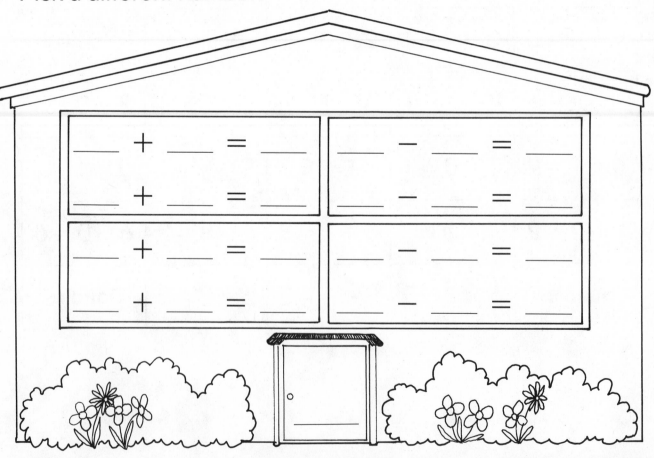

Name _____

Pasta Problems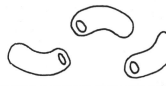

Read the story about Cathy and her family.
Use macaroni pieces to show the data.
Add or take away pieces to solve the problems.
Write a number sentence to match.

1. There are three less than ten people in my family.

2. My mom and dad have six minus one children.

3. I have three less than four sisters.

4. My sister and I have seven minus four brothers.

5. We have one more than two cats.

6. We have seven less than nine dogs.

1. $\underline{10} - \underline{3} = \underline{7}$ **2.** ___ ○ ___ □ ___

3. ___ ○ ___ □ ___   **4.** ___ ○ ___ □ ___

5. ___ ○ ___ □ ___   **6.** ___ ○ ___ □ ___

Name _____

Spin Art

You need: a friend, a spinner with numbers 11 to 18, and two different-colored crayons.

Rules: Each player chooses a color.
Take turns to spin.
Subtract 9 from the number on the spinner.
Color the same number of squares as the difference.
Color squares anywhere on the board.
Work together to color a design.

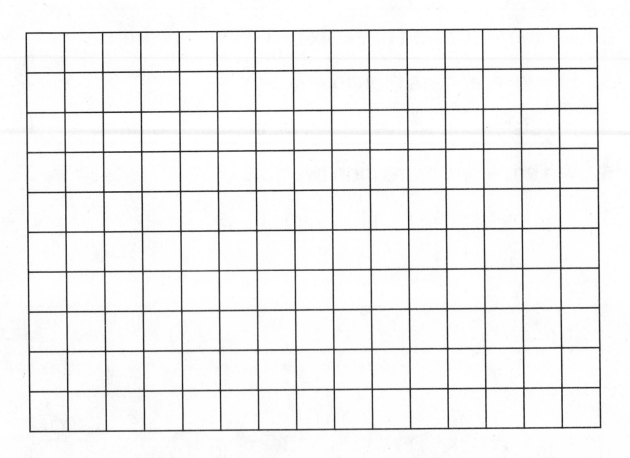

Name _____

Spin, Bubble, and Roll

You need: a friend, a spinner with the numbers 4 – 6, a number cube with the numbers 10 – 15, and a marker for each player.

Rules: Let your friend go first.

Roll the number cube and spin the spinner.

Subtract  from ⬡ .

Move that number of spaces on the game board.

The first player to reach the bottle of bubbles wins.

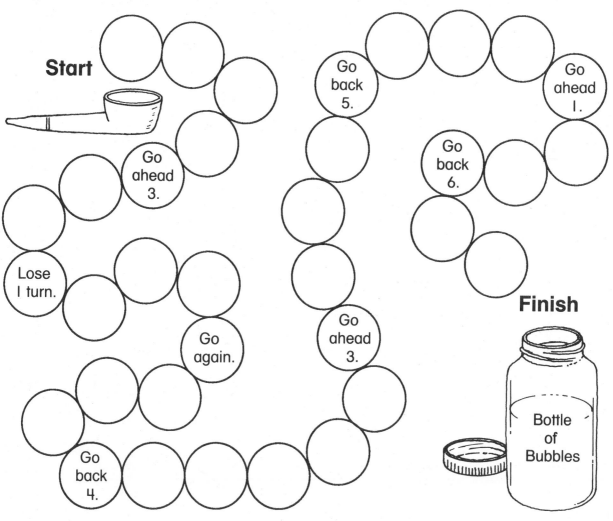

Find the Facts

Find three numbers in a row that make a subtraction fact.
Look across or down in the direction shown by the arrows.
Ring each fact. Can you find 20?

4 – 3 = 1	7	3	2	1	6	0
7 12 7	5	5	9	6	3	10
3 0 4	2	1	8	13	5	8
11 1 10	8	2	18	14	7	2
8 9 2	3	15	9	6	1	2
3 10 6	1	14	9	8	12	6
8 11 5	6	15	0	15	7	3
4 8 1	2	6	12	9	3	3
2 7 3	4	2	1	5	3	8

Name _____

Library Stories

Read the stories.
Draw an X on the **take away** stories.
Draw an O on the **compare** stories.
Write the number sentences.

1. There were
12 books in the
store window.
6 were sold.
How many
were left?

___ ___ = ___

2. The library has
5 record
players and
7 tape players.
How many are
there in all?

___ ___ = ___

3. Our class has
11 records.
Ali's class
has 6. How
many more
records do
we have?

___ ___ = ___

4. Al has 16
books. Sam
borrowed 9.
How many
does Al have
left?

___ ___ = ___

5. Ben read 3
books. Then
he read 8.
How many did
he read in all?

___ ___ = ___

6. 13 people
have library
cards. 9 do
not. How
many more
have library
cards?

___ ___ = ___

Name _____

Calculator Challenge

1. | 6 | | 7 | | 9 | | + | | − | | = |

Use each of these keys only once. Use no other keys.

Make your calculator read ⟶ | **1 0** |

Write the keys in the correct order.

_____

2. Now use these keys.

| 8 | | 4 | | 9 | | + | | − | | = |

Make your calculator read ⟶ | **1 3** |

Write what you did.

_____

3. Here is one more.

| 8 | | 7 | | 8 | | + | | − | | = |

Make your calculator read ⟶ | **9** |

Write how you did it.

_____

4. Make up your own puzzle.

Name _____

Is It True?

Write **true** if the statement is true.
Write **false** if the statement is not true.

 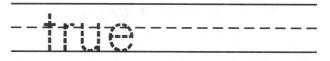

1. $10 - 5 = 11 - 6$ true

2. $16 - 7 = 18 - 9$

3. $14 - 6 = 12 - 5$

4. $13 - 7 = 12 - 6$

5. $17 - 8 = 16 - 9$

6. $12 - 8 = 11 - 7$

Change each false statement to make it true.

7. _____

8. _____

Name _____

Falling Leaves

Write a number sentence for each story.

1. Amy had 7 leaves. She found 5 more on her way home from school. How many does she have in all?

_____

2. Amy put all her leaves in a pile. Just then a big wind came along. 5 leaves blew away! How many leaves does Amy have now?

_____

3. Amy went to look for leaves in the park. She wanted to have as many leaves in all as she had before. How many leaves does Amy need to find?

_____

4. Look at the number sentences you wrote. What fact is missing from the fact family?

_____

5. Finish the story about Amy and her leaves. Write a problem to match the last number sentence.

_____
- -
_____
_____
- -
_____

A Game of More or Less

You need: a friend, a number cube with the numbers 1 to 6, 50 paper clips in a bowl, 2 counters.

Rules: Take turns. Toss the number cube.
Move the counter that number of spaces on the game board.
Read the words on the space. If they tell about addition,
take that many clips. If the words tell about subtraction,
put that many clips back in the bowl. When you reach **Finish**,
add your clips to your friend's. What is the total?

Start

and 10 more	the sum is 8	12 altogether
take 9 more	14 in all	the total is 15
find 6	put 7 back	the difference is 5
4 are added	lose 6	give 5 back
have 7 more	put 9 away	3 are lost
add 6	3 go away	and 10 less

Finish

Name _____

Guess and Measure

Find things to measure.

Pick a unit to use.

First estimate, then measure.

Fill in the chart.

Try measuring the same thing using different units of measure.

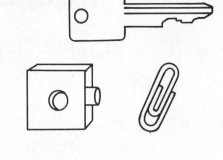

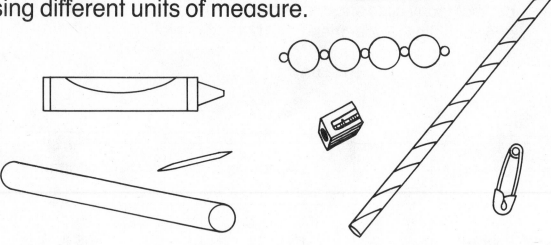

Eraser

I am measuring	I am using	I estimate	I measure
my shoe	beads		

Name _____

Sea Stars

Connect the stars in order from letters A to H.
Then draw a line between H and D.

Describe your picture. _____

Estimate the length from A to D.   estimate: _____ inches

Measure the length from A to D.   measure: _____ nearest
                                                                  inch

Estimate which lines are almost as long as A to D.

_____

Estimate which line is nearest to I inch. _____

Now measure the lines to the nearest inch to check.

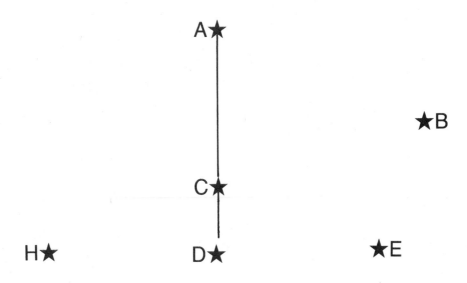

Name _____

Measuring at Home

Dear Family,
     Your child is learning about measuring in inches and making graphs. Provide an inch ruler and help your child find three items around your home that are less than 12 inches long.

Work with a family member. Find three things to measure.
Measure each item to the nearest inch.
Fill in the chart. Ask your family member to write the names of the items.

Item	Nearest Inch

Make a graph to show the data. Write the name of the item on the side of the graph.   Color one box for each inch.

Talk about what the graph tells you.
Which item is longest? Which is the shortest?

Name _____

A Long Walk

Alvin Ant can walk 1 inch each hour.
How many hours will it take him to walk
around the figure?
Hint: Use mental math. Count on to add as you measure each side.

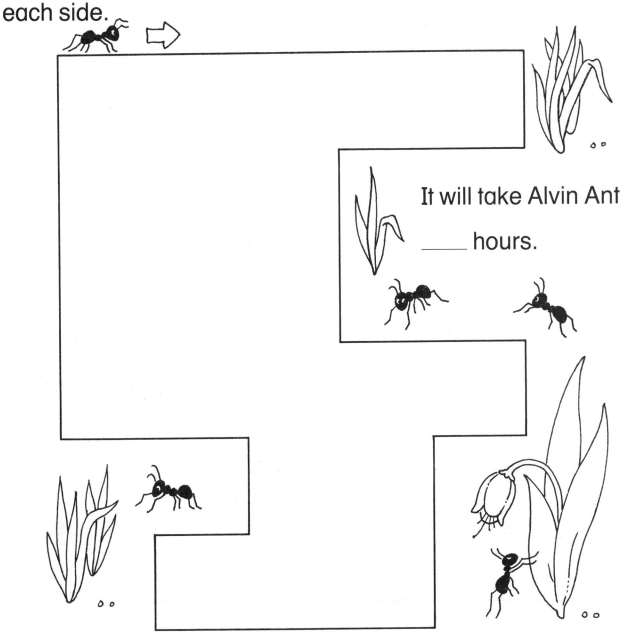

It will take Alvin Ant

_____ hours.

Name _____

Measuring Around School

Work with a group.
Put your yardsticks from end to end to measure.
Use your foot rulers to measure any feet left over.
Write each measure in yards and feet.

Remember: There are 3 feet in 1 yard.

1. The length of the classroom

_____ yards _____ feet

2. The width of the classroom

_____ yards _____ feet

3. The distance from one student's desk to the teacher's desk

_____ yards _____ feet

4. The distance from the teacher's desk to the door

_____ yards _____ feet

Measure other lengths in your classroom.
First write what you measured.
Then write the length in yards and feet.

5. _____

_____ yards _____ foot/feet

6. _____

_____ yards _____ foot/feet

Name _____

Measuring for a Party

Emma wants to make party punch.
She uses this recipe.
She has only a 1-cup measure.

```
          ·:ξ⑤ Party Punch ⑤:·. cups
3 pints pineapple juice          ____
1 quart orange juice             ____
2 pints lime juice               ____
1 pint ice cream                 ____
```

Can you help her?
Change all of the measures to cups.

REMEMBER:	2 cups = 1 pint	2 pints = 1 quart

Now use the recipe to answer the questions.

1. How many pints are there in the recipe? _____

2. How many cups of lime juice would you need to make

one half of the recipe? _____

3. Will this recipe make enough punch for 15 people

to have 1 cup each? _____

Name _____

Estimate and Weigh

Estimate what will happen to your weight.
Then use a scale to measure.

1. How much do you weigh?

Estimate: _____

Weight: _____

2. Stand on one foot. Now how much do you weigh?

Estimate: _____

Weight: _____

3. Have a friend stand on one foot. What is the weight?

Estimate: _____

Weight: _____

4. How much do you and your friend weigh together?

Estimate: _____

Weight: _____

5. How much do you weigh without your shoes on?

Estimate: _____

Weight: _____

With your coat and hat on?

Estimate: _____

Weight: _____

6. Hold some books. How much do you weigh?

Estimate: _____

Weight: _____

How much do the books weigh?

Estimate: _____

Weight: _____

Name _____

Estimating Lengths

About how long is it?

A centimeter is this long. ⊢⊣

1. Your shoe

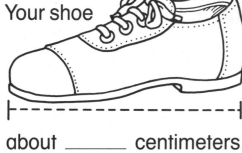

about _____ centimeters

2. Your hand

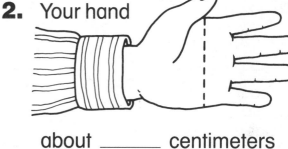

about _____ centimeters

3. A pencil

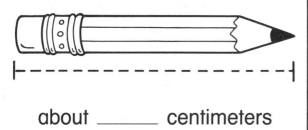

about _____ centimeters

4. Desk or table

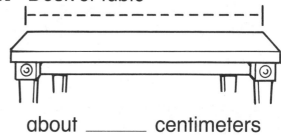

about _____ centimeters

5. Find two things. Draw them. Then tell about how long they are.

about _____ centimeters

6.

about _____ centimeters

Name _____

Measuring Friends

Cut a piece of string 1 decimeter long.
Cut a piece of string 1 meter long.
Use the strings to measure yourself.
Put a ✔ in the box on the chart that matches
each measure.

Your	Less than 1 decimeter	More than 1 decimeter	About 1 meter	More than 1 meter
finger				
leg				
arm				
waist				
height				
foot				

Now measure a friend.
Fill in the chart.

Your friend's	Less than 1 decimeter	More than 1 decimeter	About 1 meter	More than 1 meter
finger				
leg				
arm				
waist				
height				
foot				

Compare the two charts. How are they the same?
How are they different?

Put It in Order

Number the containers in order.
Start with **1** for the container that holds the least.

Which container holds about a liter? _____

Name _____

How Many Squares?

Use straight lines to draw a shape on your
paper. Count the number of squares it covers.
Exchange papers with a partner.
Estimate how many squares each other's
shape covers. Then count.

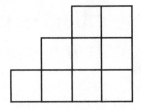

___9___ squares

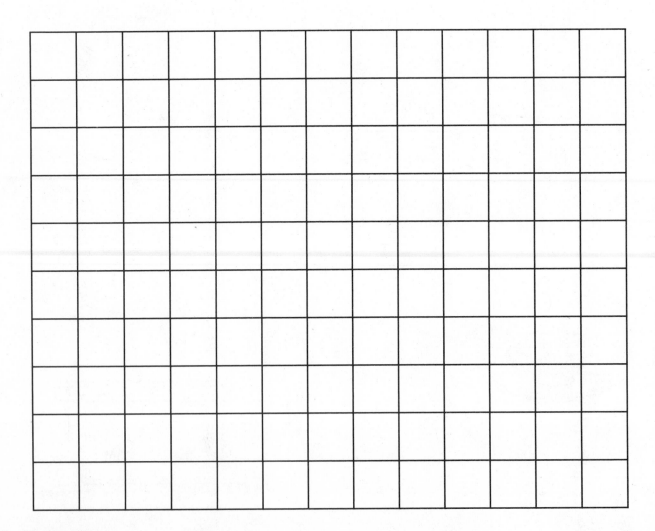

Estimate: _____ squares   Count: _____ squares
How close was your guess?

Name _____

How Many?

Count the cubes.
Complete a sentence to tell how many tens and ones.

1.

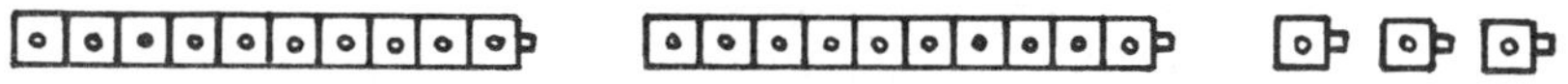

There are _____ and _____.

2.

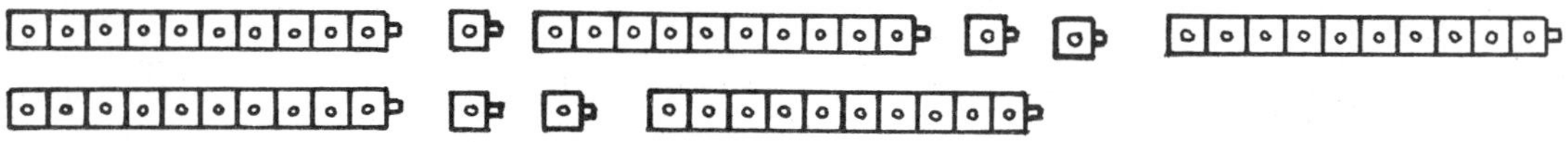

There are _____ and _____.

3.

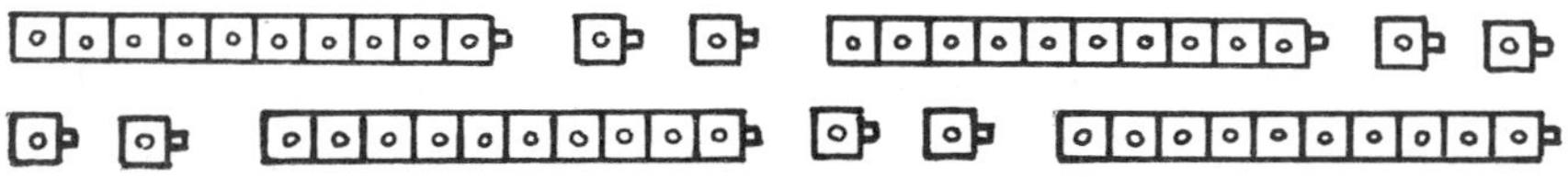

There are _____ and _____.

4.

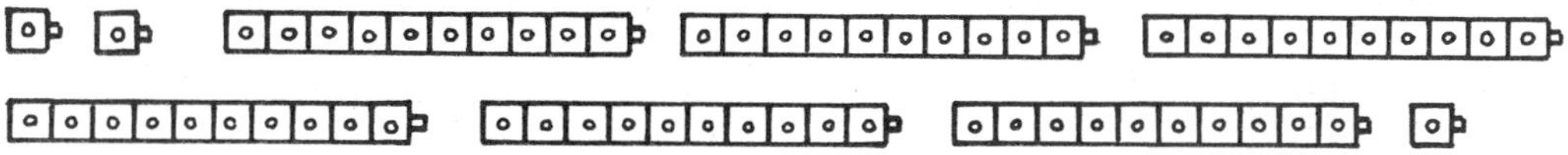

There are _____ and _____.

5.

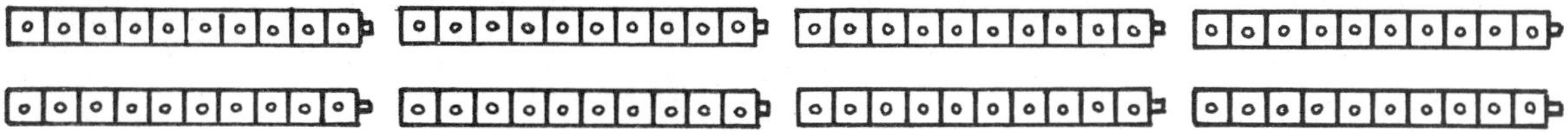

There are _____ and _____.

Name _____

Guess and Count

Estimate how many tens and ones without counting. Write the numbers. Then ring sets of tens. Count tens and ones to find out how many there really are.
Write the numbers.

	Tens	Ones
Estimate ⟶		
Count ⟶		

	Tens	Ones
Estimate ⟶		
Count ⟶		

	Tens	Ones
Estimate ⟶		
Count ⟶		

	Tens	Ones
Estimate ⟶		
Count ⟶		

Use with text pages 139–140.

Name _____

On Target

Each ★ shows where a dart hit.
Write the score.
Then write the word name.

1.

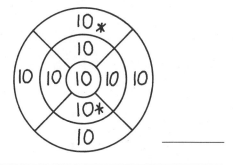

_____ _____

_____

2.

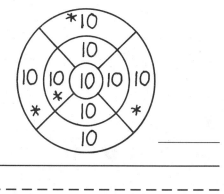

_____ _____

_____

3.

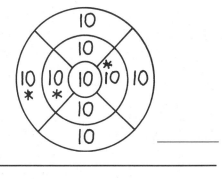

_____ _____

_____

4.

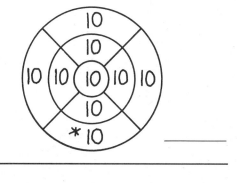

_____ _____

_____

Make ★ s to show the score.

5.

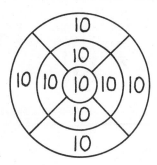

70

6.

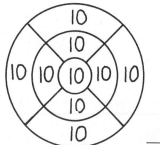

60

Ten and One

Work with a partner.

☐☐☐☐☐☐☐☐☐ ☐ → I I

Show I ten and I one.

Circle the number on the chart.

Add I more ten and I more one. Circle that number.

Add a ten and a one each time.

Take turns showing the tens and ones and circling the numbers.

Ⓞ	I	2	3	4	5	6	7	8	9
10	II	12	13	14	15	16	17	18	19
20	21	22	23	24	25	26	27	28	29
30	31	32	33	34	35	36	37	38	39
40	41	42	43	44	45	46	47	48	49
50	51	52	53	54	55	56	57	58	59
60	61	62	63	64	65	66	67	68	69
70	71	72	73	74	75	76	77	78	79
80	81	82	83	84	85	86	87	88	89
90	91	92	93	94	95	96	97	98	99

Talk about the pattern you made.

Play again. Start with a different number.

Name _____

Write the Data

Read each story.
Fill in the missing data so the story is true.
Write the matching subtraction sentence to check.

1. Brian ran ____ miles.

Fran ran ____ miles.
Brian ran 5 more miles
than Fran.

_____

2. Lisa jumped ____ feet.

Kevin jumped ____ feet.
Lisa jumped 3 more
feet than Kevin.

_____

3. Tom ran ____ laps.

Roz ran ____ laps.
Roz ran 7 more laps
than Tom.

_____

4. There were ____
swimming races. There

were ____ running
races. There were
4 more running races.

_____

5. Our team won ____
blue ribbons and

____ red ribbons.
We won 2 more blue
ribbons.

_____

6. This year there were

____ events. Next year

there will be ____
events. There will be
I more event next year.

_____

Name _____

Do Not Spend It All

What coins are left?

These are the coins you have.	This is what you buy.	What coins do you have left?
1.	22¢	_____ dimes _____ pennies
2.	12¢	_____ dimes _____ pennies
3.	34¢	_____ dimes _____ pennies
4.	33¢	_____ dimes _____ pennies
5.	56¢	_____ dimes _____ pennies

Name _____

Crossnumber Puzzle

Dear Family,
   In our math book we just studied the reading and writing of 2-digit numbers. Have your child read the number names aloud before writing the numbers in the puzzle. Then work together to write the clues for the second puzzle. Help with spelling as needed.

Read the clues. Write the numbers.

A	B	■	C	D
■	E	F	■	
■	■	G	H	■
I		■	J	K
	■	■	■	

Across
A. forty-four
C. twenty-three
E. twenty-nine
G. sixty-seven
I. sixteen
J. eighty-three

Down
B. forty-two
D. thirty-one
F. ninety-six
H. seventy-eight
I. thirteen
K. thirty-nine

Write the clues for the puzzle. Use extra paper.

A 6	B 5	■	C 4	D 2
■	E 3	F 9	■	6
■	■	G 1	H 6	■
I 8	6	■	J 4	K 7
3	■	■	■	2

Name _____

Press and Write

Use your 🖩 . Press the keys in order.
Write the numbers you see.

1. | ON/C | **9** | **4** | **+** | **1** | **=** | **=** | **=** | **=** | **=** | **=** |

_____ _95_ _____ _____ _____ _____

2. | ON/C | **9** | **8** | **+** | **1** | **=** | **=** | **=** | **=** | **=** | **=** |

_____ _____ _____ _____ _____ _____

3. | ON/C | **1** | **0** | **3** | **–** | **1** | **=** | **=** | **=** | **=** | **=** | **=** |

_____ _____ _____ _____ _____ _____

4. | ON/C | **4** | **0** | **+** | **1** | **0** | **=** | **=** | **=** | **=** | **=** | **=** |

_____ _____ _____ _____ _____ _____

5. Say the numbers with a friend.
   Talk about the patterns.

Name _____

Fair Shares

Read each problem. Make the same number in each group.
Use counters to find the answer.

1. There are 18 cards.
Dan and Lynn want to play.
How many cards should
each one get?

_____

2. There are 24 marbles.
3 friends want to play.
How many marbles
should each one get?

_____

3. There are 12 books.
There are 3 shelves.
How many books should
go on each shelf?

_____

4. There are 20 pancakes.
There are 4 plates.
How many pancakes
should go on each plate?

_____

5. There are 16 chairs.
There are 4 tables.
How many chairs should
be put at each table?

_____

6. There are 18 students.
We need 3 groups.
How many students
should be in each group?

_____

7. There are 24 nuts and
4 squirrels. How many
nuts for each?

_____

8. There are 14 carrots
and 2 rabbits. How
many carrots for each?

_____

Name _____

Hidden Numbers

Play with a partner. Player 1 takes 5 counters and covers
5 numbers.
Player 2 tells what numbers are hidden.
Player 1 writes the numbers on a piece of paper.
Both players check by taking off the counters.
Now Player 2 covers 5 numbers.

1	2	3	4	5	6	7	8	9	10
11	12	13	14	15	16	17	18	19	20
21	22	23	24	25	26	27	28	29	30
31	32	33	34	35	36	37	38	39	40
41	42	43	44	45	46	47	48	49	50
51	52	53	54	55	56	57	58	59	60
61	62	63	64	65	66	67	68	69	70
71	72	73	74	75	76	77	78	79	80
81	82	83	84	85	86	87	88	89	90
91	92	93	94	95	96	97	98	99	100

Name _____

Find Rusty's Bone

Start at number 34. Color the number that comes next. You can go left, right, up, or down.

34	35	53	77	47	97	39	18	85	60	17	69	46	29	94	55
43	36	31	43	49	34	54	26	96	52	16	80	71	98	83	28
67	37	52	41	42	43	44	47	61	15	79	45	12	54	99	27
48	38	39	40	51	25	45	54	97	40	70	95	82	93	26	57
28	62	76	61	92	48	46	64	76	51	13	86	30	53	56	38
86	41	63	60	15	51	47	74	14	81	44	78	43	25	93	72
62	34	60	40	50	49	48	60	69	55	40	26	36	46	56	69
78	85	48	15	51	34	26	49	42	47	78	62	63	64	65	66
84	22	98	25	52	56	72	84	37	85	72	61	36	32	85	67
35	80	90	35	53	54	55	56	57	58	59	60	29	67	86	68
62	91	49	59	38	44	43	65	75	68	63	46	44	38	96	69
79	21	91	33	58	66	50	48	65	54	47	74	73	72	71	70
69	89	82	90	19	68	57	53	72	31	57	75	37	27	67	92
36	66	20	50	90	73	24	81	87	77	67	76	57	92	75	56
63	83	64	87	45	67	74	52	46	71	84	77	85	28	28	38
64	43	32	44	68	23	88	32	41	40	68	78	79	80	81	82
37	65	88	51	67	89	76	42	70	75	27	19	97	64	37	83

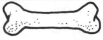

An Amazing Trip

Help the kangaroo hop through the maze.

Use your 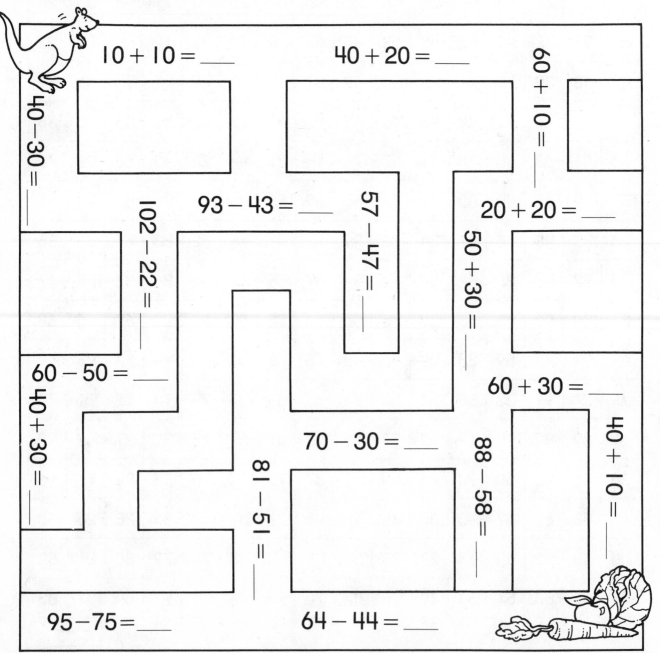 to fill in all the blanks. Then color the path of addition sentences that lead to the food.

10 + 10 = ___

40 + 20 = ___

60 + 10 = ___

40 − 30 = ___

93 − 43 = ___

57 − 47 = ___

20 + 20 = ___

102 − 22 = ___

50 + 30 = ___

60 − 50 = ___

40 + 30 = ___

70 − 30 = ___

60 + 30 = ___

88 − 58 = ___

40 + 10 = ___

81 − 51 = ___

95 − 75 = ___

64 − 44 = ___

Which Bookworm?

In each pair of numbers, which number is greater?
Find that number on the chart and color it red.

17, 10	44, 34	75, 65
16, 26	23, 53	86, 68
33, 35	64, 46	79, 97

1	2	3	4	5	6	7	8	9	10
11	12	13	14	15	16	17	18	19	20
21	22	23	24	25	26	27	28	29	30
31	32	33	34	35	36	37	38	39	40
41	42	43	44	45	46	47	48	49	50
51	52	53	54	55	56	57	58	59	60
61	62	63	64	65	66	67	68	69	70
71	72	73	74	75	76	77	78	79	80
81	82	83	84	85	86	87	88	89	90
91	92	93	94	95	96	97	98	99	100

Which bookworm did you draw? _____ greater than   less than

Name _____

Sign Sense

Follow the sentence.
Write > or < in each ○.

1. 95 ○ 63 ○ 54 ○ 82 ○ 99
2. 33 ○ 25 ○ 76 ○ 66 ○ 87
3. 91 ○ 72 ○ 60 ○ 46 ○ 25
4. 44 ○ 21 ○ 15 ○ 76 ○ 59

Follow the signs. Write a 2-digit number in each ☐.

5. 86 ⊘ ☐ ⊘ ☐ ⊘ ☐
6. 45 ⊘ ☐ ⊘ ☐ ⊘ ☐
7. 99 ⊘ ☐ ⊘ ☐ ⊘ ☐ ⊘ ☐
8. 16 ⊘ ☐ ⊘ ☐ ⊘ ☐ ⊘ ☐

Skip Counting

Dear Family,
    We have just learned to skip count by 2s, 3s, and 4s. Help your child practice by playing this game. You will need a dime and pencil and paper to write the counting patterns.

Turn this page upside down. Take turns.

Put the dime on the Name line.

Flick it with your finger so it lands on the game board.

If your dime lands on a number in the counting pattern

▷ for 2s = 1 point   ▷ for 3s = 1 point

▷ for 2s and 4s = 2 points   ▷ for 2s and 3s = 3 points

▷ for 2s, 3s, and 4s = 4 points

The first player to get 25 points wins.

28	10	33	22	32
30	21	24	20	26
	14	16	15	
14	9	18	4	8
27	12	2	6	3

Name _____

Quarterback

Count by 5s to connect the dots.

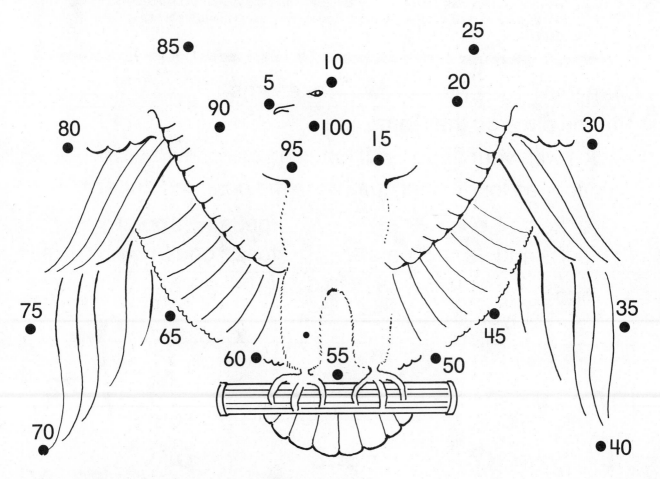

What bird did you draw? _____

This bird is on what coin? _____

On another piece of paper, draw your own bird picture.
Decide where to put the dots.
Write the numbers, counting by 5s.
Ask a friend to connect the dots.
Remember to give your friend helpful hints if needed.

Name _____

Hop, Skip, and Jump

Dear Family,
    Your child is learning the order of numbers, first through tenth. Follow the directions to finish the game board together, then play the game. You will need a number cube to tell how many spaces to move, and a marker for each player.

1. Write **go back 1** on the 4th, 7th, and 12th spaces.

2. Write **go ahead 2** on the 8th, 17th, and 21st spaces.

3. Write **lose 1 turn** on the 11th and 24th spaces.

Roll the number cube and move that many spaces.
Follow the directions in the space.
The first player to land on FINISH wins.

START

Take giant steps around the room.

Hop on 1 foot 10 times.

Skip around the room.

Stand on 1 foot and recite a poem.

Touch your toes 5 times.

FINISH

Tip-toe to the door and back.

Jump around the room.

Addison-Wesley | All Rights Reserved

Name _____

Line Up

Read the clues.
Write each name to show the order.

Ellen

Anna

David   Craig   Betty

Anna is first in line.
David is between Anna and Ellen.
Ellen is not fourth or fifth in line.
Craig is not last.
Which students are 2nd, 3rd, 4th, and last in line?

Anna _____ _____ _____ _____
first   second   third   fourth   last

Name _____

How Long Will It Take?

> Dear Family,
>   Your child is learning about time in 5-minute intervals. Help your child with this activity to provide practice in predicting how long a task will take.

Look at this list of jobs.

brush my teeth	eat breakfast	walk the dog
get dressed	clear my dishes	travel to school
make my bed	feed the cat	set the table
clean up my room	feed the dog	take a bath

How long do you think each one takes?
Choose one job to finish each sentence below.
Ask a family member to time you. Do the job.
Then write the number of minutes the job took.

1. In 5 MINUTES I think I can _____.

It took ____ minutes.

2. In 10 MINUTES I think I can _____.

It took ____ minutes.

3. In 15 MINUTES I think I can _____.

It took ____ minutes.

4. In 30 MINUTES I think I can _____.

It took ____ minutes.

Name _____

What Time Is It?

Make the clock show the given time.

1.

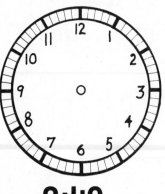

10:15

2.

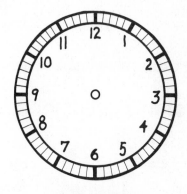

6:20

3.

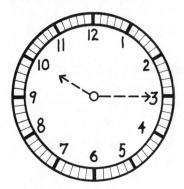

2:40

4.

12:45

5.

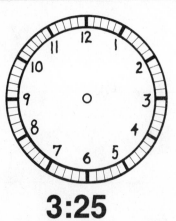

3:25

6.

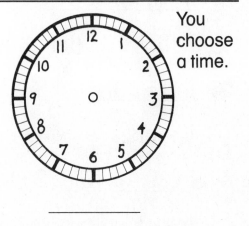

You choose a time.

_____

Name _____

What Do You Think?

Think about the minute hand only.

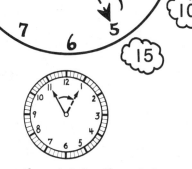

From the 2 to the
5 is 15 minutes.

How many minutes?

1.

From the 7 to the 11 is

20 minutes.

2.

From the 11 to the 1 is

_____ minutes.

3.

From the 2 to the 10 is

_____ minutes.

4.

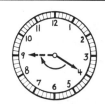

From the 4 to the 9 is

_____ minutes.

5.

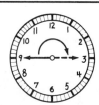

From the 9 to the 3 is

_____ minutes.

6.

From the 7 to the 5 is

_____ minutes.

Name _____

Astro Time

Look at the dots next to each time and end time.
Begin by thinking of 12:00.
What will the end time be 1 hour later?
Put your pencil on the dot at 1:00.
Draw a line to the end time 30 minutes later.
Draw a line to the next end time.
Keep doing this.

• 11:00
  End: 1 hour
  later

• 1:00
  End: 30 minutes
  later

• 2:00
  End: 1 hour
  later

• 4:30
  End: 1 hour
  30 minutes later

• 3:30
  End: 1 hour
  later

• 1:30
  End: 2 hours
  later

• 5:00
  End: 1 hour
  later

• 6:00
  End: 7 hours
  later

What did you draw? _____

Name _____

Calendar Memories

Look at a calendar with your family.

Talk about the things your family does each month.

Think about what dates are important to your family.

Write a sentence or draw a picture to explain what each month means to your family.

January	February	March	April
May	June	July	August
September	October	November	December

Probability

You need: 2 number cubes with numbers 1 to 6, crayons.

Rules: Roll 2 number cubes. Name the sum.
If the sum is even, color a square in the Even Sum pyramid.
If the sum is odd, color a square in the Odd Sum pyramid.
If you roll doubles, color a square in the Doubles pyramid
<u>and</u> in the Even Sum pyramid.
Keep rolling the number cubes until you have filled in one pyramid.
Predict which pyramid you will fill first:

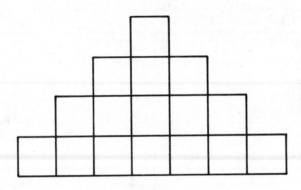

Doubles

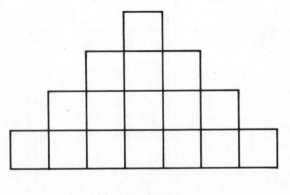

Even Sum

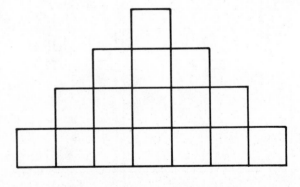

Odd Sum

Name _____

Price the Toys

How much is each toy?
Write the amount on the tag.

Dimes	Nickels	Pennies	
1	2	3	28¢
2	1	4	¢
1	1	2	¢
3	0	3	¢
2	3	0	¢
3	2	4	¢

Name _____

4-Coin Bingo

You need: a partner, punchout coins, a game board
for each player, and a spinner.

Rules: Take turns. Spin the arrow.
If the arrow points to a dime, put a dime
punchout on the board.
Do this for pennies, nickels, and quarters, too.
The object is to get 4 of the same coins
in a row on your own board.
A **row** means up and down, across, or on a slant.

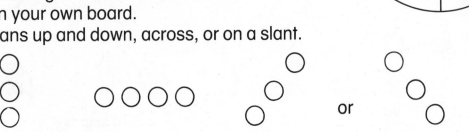

Play until someone has 4 of the same coins in a row.

To win, you must add the 4 coins correctly.

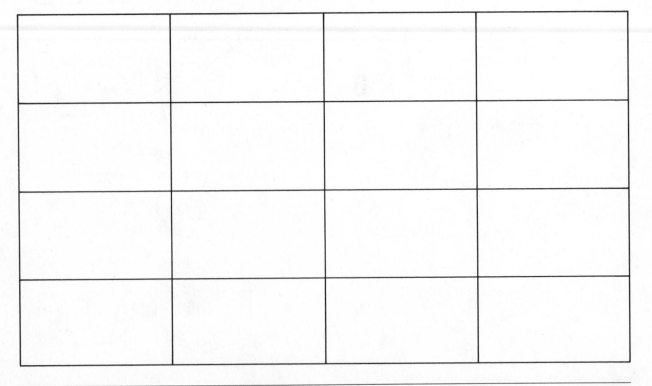

Name _____

Savings and Loan

Dear Family,
   Your child is learning to recognize and count money. To play this game you will need $1 in pennies, nickels, dimes, and quarters, and a marker for each player.

Rules: To start, players each get 50¢.
Each player chooses a game board and puts a marker on **Start**.
Flip a penny. If it lands heads up, move 2 spaces.
If it lands tails up, move 1 space. Follow the directions
on the space. Take turns until both players reach **Finish**.
The player with the most money in the bank wins.

Start

Put a nickel in your bank.	Put 2 dimes in your friend's bank.	Put 2 dimes in your bank.	Put a quarter in your friend's bank.	Get a quarter from your friend's bank.	Put a half dollar in your bank.
Put a dime in your bank.	Put a nickel in your bank.				Put a quarter in your friend's bank.
Put a nickel in your friend's bank.	**Finish**				Put a nickel in your friend's bank.
Put a quarter in your friend's bank.				**Finish**	Put a dime in your bank.
Put a half dollar in your bank.	Get a quarter from your friend's bank.	Put a quarter in your friend's bank.	Put 2 dimes in your bank.	Put a nickel in your bank. / Put 2 dimes in your friend's bank.	Put a nickel in your bank.

Start

Name _____

Coin Chart

Work with a partner. Use your coin punchouts.
Decide which coins to use to show the different
ways to make each amount.
Draw the coins you choose like this: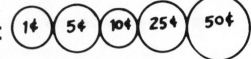

Remember: Build on each other's good ideas.

26¢	37¢
4 coins:	4 coins:
5 coins:	5 coins:
6 coins:	6 coins:

41¢	66¢
4 coins:	4 coins:
5 coins:	5 coins:
6 coins:	6 coins:

Use with text pages 199–200.

What's the Score?

You need: a partner, a number cube, and a spinner.

Rules: Take turns. Write a team name on the scoreboard below.
Spin the spinner and roll the number cube.
The number cube tells the number of runs for your team.
If the spinner lands on **Even,** write the
number of runs in an even-numbered
inning—2, 4, 6, or 8.
If the spinner lands on **Odd,** write the
number of runs in an odd-numbered
inning—1, 3, 5, 7, or 9.
If you have filled in all the even
innings and the spinner lands on Even,
you lose the turn.
Total all the runs for the 9 innings.
The team with the most runs wins.

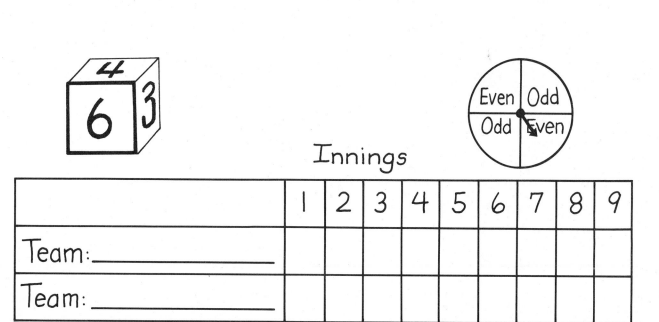

		1	2	3	4	5	6	7	8	9
Team:_____										
Team:_____										

Name _____

The Bigger the Better: A Game for One

You need: 2 number cubes, base-ten blocks.

Rules: Roll the 2 number cubes.
Write the larger 2-digit number you can make on the first line
in the Game 1 box below.
Then roll just 1 number cube.
Add it to the big number and find your score.
Use base-ten blocks to check your scores.
Take 3 turns for each game.
Play 2 games.
Ring the highest score in each game with one color.
Ring the lowest game score with another color.

Game 1				**Score**
1. ___ ___	+	___	=	___ ___
2. ___ ___	+	___	=	___ ___
3. ___ ___	+	___	=	___ ___

Game 2				**Score**
1. ___ ___	+	___	=	___ ___
2. ___ ___	+	___	=	___ ___
3. ___ ___	+	___	=	___ ___

Snack Time

Snack Bar

milk 20¢   apple 40¢   crackers 50¢

juice 30¢   banana 10¢   muffin 60¢

Use the sign to solve the problems.

1. Amy bought milk and a banana. How much did she spend? _____

2. Jeff bought a muffin and juice. How much did he spend? _____

3. Gregg bought an apple. He spent 60¢. What else did he buy?

_____

- - - - - - - - - - - - - -

_____

4. Sandy bought crackers. She spent 90¢. What else did she buy?

_____

- - - - - - - - - - - - - -

_____

5. Pablo bought an apple and a drink. He spent 70¢. What drink did he buy?

_____

- - - - - - - - - - - - - -

_____

6. Anna bought a snack and milk. She spent 30¢. What snack did she buy?

_____

- - - - - - - - - - - - - -

_____

7. Don spent 80¢. What three things did he buy?

_____

- -

_____

Spin a Sum

Play with a partner.
Use spinners and a different color crayon for each of you.

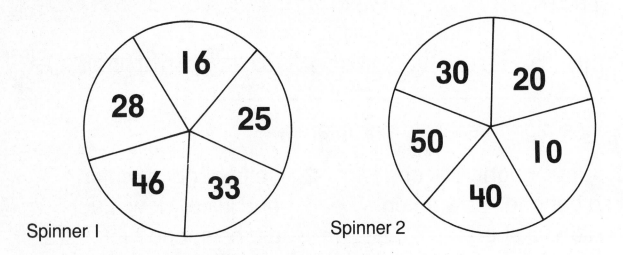

Spinner 1   Spinner 2

Spin the first spinner to find the start number.
Spin the second spinner and count on the number of tens.
Color the sum.
Now your partner spins for tens, counts on from the start number,
and colors that sum.
Spin again to change the start number.
Keep playing until one of you colors a whole row of sums.

38	36	43	66	78
83	75	46	35	26
48	53	56	45	73
63	58	65	76	55
96	68	86	56	66

Name _____

Crossnumbers

Add the pair of numbers.
When you make another ten, write the sum in its numbered space in the crossnumber puzzle. The first one is done for you.

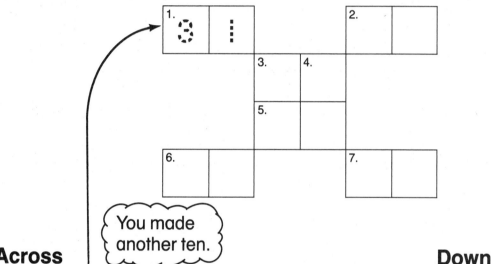

You made another ten.

Across

1.
$$13 \quad 19$$
$$+13 \quad +12$$
$$\overline{26} \quad \overline{31}$$

2.
$$14 \quad 10$$
$$+18 \quad +12$$

3.
$$12 \quad 16$$
$$+12 \quad +17$$

5.
$$19 \quad 16$$
$$+ 4 \quad + 2$$

6.
$$28 \quad 11$$
$$+ 2 \quad +11$$

7.
$$14 \quad 11$$
$$+14 \quad + 9$$

Down

3.
$$18 \quad 6$$
$$+14 \quad +2$$

4.
$$44 \quad 17$$
$$+22 \quad +16$$

Name _____

Estimation Steps

You need: a friend, 2 counters, a number cube, and a spinner like this:

Rules: Take turns. Begin at **Start.**
Roll the number cube. Move that many spaces on the game board. If the space says **+ spinner,** spin the spinner. Estimate the sum of the number on the spinner and the number in your space. If the estimate is less than 50, go down the slide. If the estimate is more than 50, go up the steps. The first player to reach **Home** wins. You must land exactly on Home to win. If the number rolled is more than the spaces left on the board, you lose a turn.

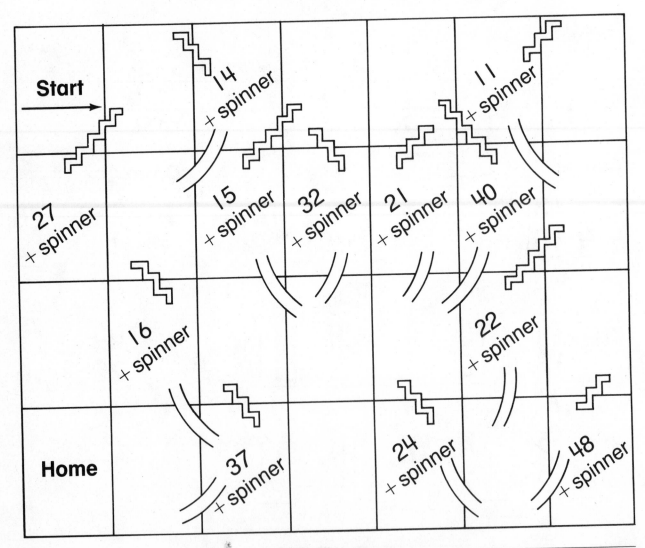

Same Sum Game

Dear Family,
    We have just completed a lesson on finding different addends to make the same sum. Play the game below with your child. Have him or her show the addition on another piece of paper.

Take turns with a family member.

Choose a number from 10 to 36.

The first player finds 2 addends in the chart to make that sum.

The second player finds two other addends to make the same sum.

10	7	14	19	5
3	9	6	12	11
25	13	16	15	11
15	8	2	20	10

Play again. Pick another number from 10 to 36.

This time player 2 goes first.

Keep playing as long as you wish.

Name _____

At My House

Draw a picture of a room in your house.

To describe your picture, finish the sentences. Write one addition sentence and one subtraction sentence.

1. There are _____ _____
    (number)   (item)

   and _____ _____.
       (number)   (item)

   How many are there in all?

   ____ $\oplus$ ____ $\boxed{=}$ ____

2. There are more _____
                                        (item)

   than _____.
                  (item)

   How many more are there?

   ____ $\ominus$ ____ $\boxed{=}$ ____

Name _____

Estimate the Sums

Add the ones.
Think about whether you can trade 10 ones for 1 ten.
Ring the better estimate for the sum.
Use blocks to check.

1.

$$\begin{array}{r} 15 \\ +\ 3 \\ \hline \end{array}$$

more than 20

less than 20

$$\begin{array}{r} 15 \\ +\ 6 \\ \hline \end{array}$$

more than 20

less than 20

$$\begin{array}{r} 14 \\ +\ 7 \\ \hline \end{array}$$

more than 20

less than 20

2.

$$\begin{array}{r} 16 \\ +\ 8 \\ \hline \end{array}$$

more than 20

less than 20

$$\begin{array}{r} 17 \\ +\ 2 \\ \hline \end{array}$$

more than 20

less than 20

$$\begin{array}{r} 13 \\ +\ 9 \\ \hline \end{array}$$

more than 20

less than 20

3.

$$\begin{array}{r} 28 \\ +\ 4 \\ \hline \end{array}$$

more than 30

less than 30

$$\begin{array}{r} 25 \\ +\ 4 \\ \hline \end{array}$$

more than 30

less than 30

$$\begin{array}{r} 26 \\ +\ 7 \\ \hline \end{array}$$

more than 30

less than 30

Name _____

Clothespins and Toothpicks

You need: 1 or more friends, 18 clothespins, and 18 toothpicks.
Rules: Use the clothespins to make tens.
              Use the toothpicks to make ones.
              Make up an addition problem.

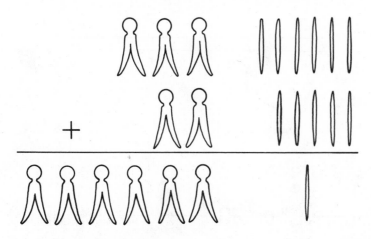

Trade
10 toothpicks
for 1 clothespin.

Ask your friend to solve it using clothespins
and toothpicks.
Check your friend's work.
Give 2 points for a correct answer.
Take turns.
The first player to get 10 points wins.

Points for You	Points for Your Friend

Name _____

Least to Greatest

Work with a friend.

You need a tens spinner labeled 1 – 4 tens
and a ones number cube labeled 4 – 9.

Take turns.

Spin the spinner and toss the cube
to make two 2-digit numbers.

Write the numbers in a chart.

Add.

Do this 4 times.

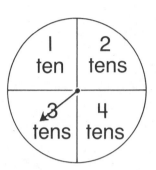

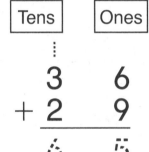

Tens	Ones
3	6
+ 2	9
6	5

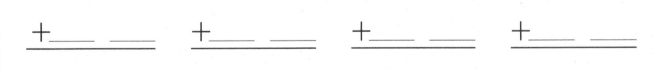

Compare the sums.

Write them from least to greatest.

_____ _____ _____ _____

Name _____

Crossnumber Puzzle Fun

Solve the problems below to fill in the puzzle.

1 5	2 2			3	4
5				6	
		7	8		
		9			
10	11			12	13
14				15	

Across
1. 27 + 25
3. 9 and 9
5. 6 tens
6. 33, 34, 35, □
7. 18 + 19
9. 6 ones, 2 tens
10. 19 + 28
12. 35 + 27
14. 6 + 9
15. 5 + 40

Down
1. 49 + 7
2. 6 + 14
3. 7 + 6
4. 54 + 32
7. 29 + 3
8. 75, □, 77
10. the number after 40
11. 49 + 26
12. 4 ones, 6 tens
13. 5, 10, 15, 20, □

Use with text pages 231–232.

Name _____

Estimating Sums About Money

This is how Sarah worked it out.

25¢ + 1¢ = __26__ ¢ or 25¢ + 5¢ = __30__ ¢ or
25¢ + 10¢ = __35__ ¢ or 25¢ + 25¢ = __50__ ¢ or
25¢ + 50¢ = __75__ ¢

Do this with a friend. Use your coin punchouts to help.
Write the amount of the last coin in the circle.

1. Suzanne has: ( ) .

She has about 30¢. What is the other coin?

---

2. Scott has: ( ) .

He has about 60¢. What is the other coin?

---

3. Charley has: ( ) .

He has about 40¢. What is the other coin?

Name _____

Sum It Up

Dear Family Member,
    Help your child practice adding 2-digit numbers. You will need 2 sets of number cards marked 0 – 5. Small pieces of paper are fine.

Take turns. Place the number cards face down.
Pick 2 cards. Use the numbers to write the <u>smallest</u>
2-digit number you can. Do this again.
Find the sum of your two numbers. The sum is your score.
Write it below. In each round, add your new sum to your
score to make a new score. The game ends when one
player's score reaches 100.

Player 1		**Player 2**	
Scores		Scores	
___ → ___		___ → ___	
+ ___ + ___		+ ___ + ___	
= ___ = ___		= ___ = ___	
+ ___ + ___		+ ___ + ___	
= ___ = ___		= ___ = ___	
+ ___ + ___		+ ___ + ___	
= ___ = ___		= ___ = ___	

Name _____

Washing Dishes

Here is a way to earn a large amount of money in only 12 days. Agree to wash the dishes for 12 days in a row. Charge 1¢ the first day, and each day after that charge twice as much as the day before. Use your calculator to find out how much you will earn each day.

Day 1 ____1____

Day 2 ____2____

Day 3 _____

Day 4 _____

Day 5 _____

Day 6 _____

Day 7 _____

Day 8 _____

Day 9 _____

Day 10 _____

Day 11 _____

Day 12 _____

Add the amounts for all 12 days. _____
Turn your paper upside down.

Did you figure out you would earn 2048¢ on the twelfth day? And 4095¢ in all? That is the same as $40.95 — more than 40 dollars!

Name _____

Data Search

Use mental math, paper and pencil, or a calculator to solve.
Finish the sentence.

	juice	35 ¢
	apple	30 ¢
	muffin	60 ¢

1.

Ann spent 95¢ in all.

She bought _____.

Mr. Reed's class:	26 students
Mrs. Rivera's class:	27 students
Miss Rice's class:	32 students

2. Two classes went to the zoo.
53 children went in all.
The classes that went to the zoo are _____

_____.

3.

24 miles — Fairview — Hope — 42 miles — Lakeville — 16 miles — Trent

The Chong family drove 58 miles in all.

They drove from _____.

4. Will read 2 books.
He read 163 pages in all.

 Freckle Juice 40 pages
 Arthur's Pen Pal 64 pages
 Beezus and Ramona 123 pages

Will read _____

_____.

Name _____

Go, Go, Go Fish

You need: a friend, a bowl, 18 paper clips, a horseshoe magnet, string, and a ruler.
Make 18 paper fish.

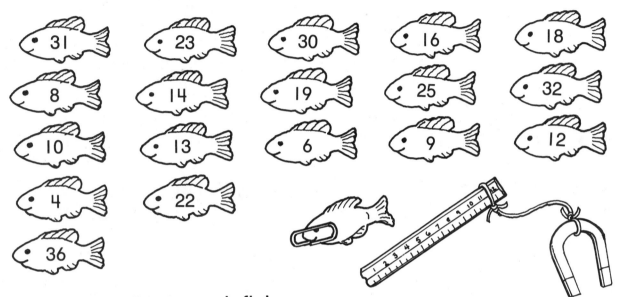

Put a paper clip on each fish.
Put all the fish in the bowl.
Make a fishing pole.

Rules: Take turns. Use the fishing pole to catch 3 fish.
Add the numbers on the fish to find the sum.
You get: 1 point if the sum is even.
            1 point if the sum is odd.
            2 points if you traded.
            3 points if the sum ends in zero.
Then put the 3 fish back in the bowl.
After 5 turns, the player with the most points wins.

Name _____

Ball Toss Game

You throw 3 balls at the board
and try to get them in the holes.
Each hole is worth a
different number of points.

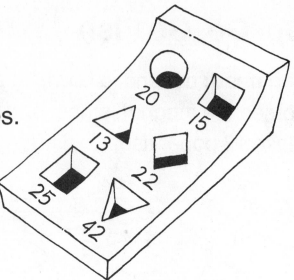

Use Guess and Check to solve. Write the answers.

1. Lee scored 75 points.
He threw all 3 balls into
the same hole. In which
hole did Lee throw the
balls?

_____

2. Trina scored 75 points.
She threw the ball into
3 different holes. In
which holes did she
throw the balls?

_____

3. David scored 57 points.
He threw the ball into
3 different holes. In
which holes did he
throw the balls?

_____

4. Rita scored 68 points.
2 of the balls went into
the same hole. In which
holes did she throw
the balls?

_____

5. What are two different ways you could get a score of 72?

_____ and _____

Manipulatives

Manipulatives 12-1

Name _____

Building Towers

Work with a partner.
Take turns following the directions to build a tower.

1. Build a tower.
Use 2 cubes and
1 cylinder.

2. Build a tower.
Use 3 cubes, 1 cylinder,
and 1 cone.

3. Build a tower.
Use 3 cylinders and
2 rectangular prisms.

4. Build a tower.
Use 2 rectangular prisms,
2 cubes, and 1 pyramid.

5. Build a tower.
Use 1 triangular
prism, 1 rectangular
prism, and 2 cubes.

6. Build a tower.
Use 3 cylinders,
1 triangular prism,
and 1 pyramid.

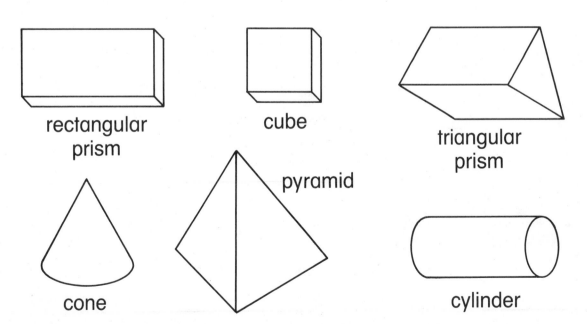

rectangular prism

cube

triangular prism

pyramid

cone

cylinder

Talk about how your towers are the same or different.

Name _____

What Is My Name?

Look at the pattern for each solid figure.
Write the name of the solid you could make from
the pattern.

1.

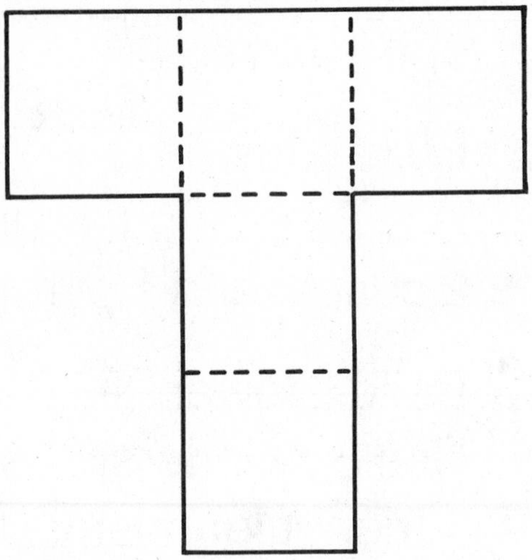

_____

2.

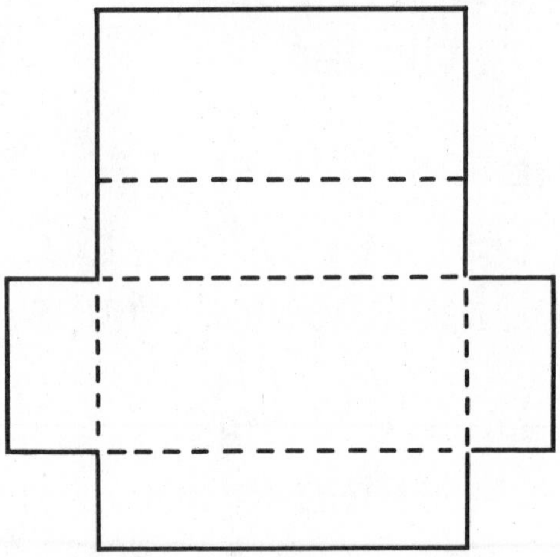

_____

3.

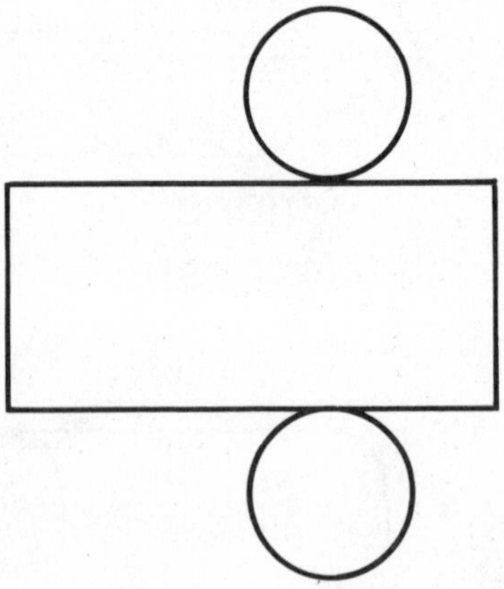

_____

4.

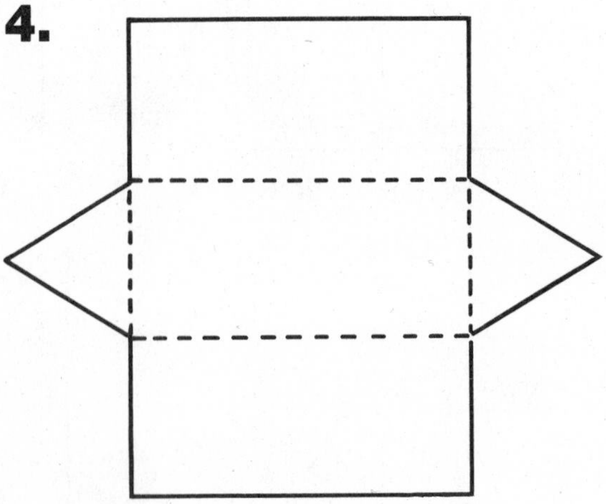

_____

Name _____

Shapes All Around

Dear Family,
   We have just finished a geometry lesson on drawing plane figures from real-world objects. Work with your child to discover things in your home that you can trace to make the shapes on the chart. You may also provide your child with pictures from magazines or newspapers to cut.

Find things you can draw around to make these shapes.
Make a picture graph.

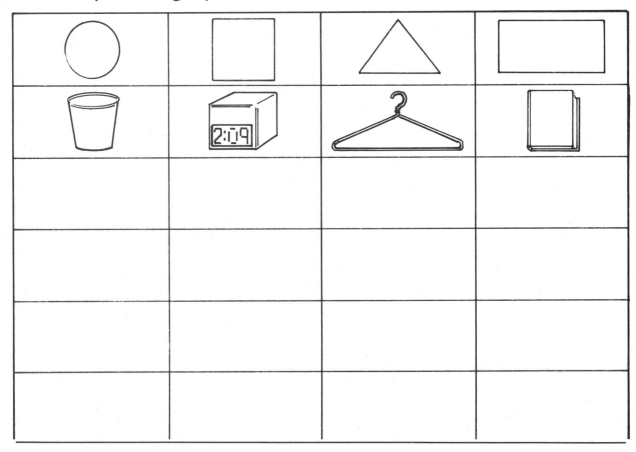

Talk about the graph.
Which shapes were easiest to find?
Which shapes were hardest to find?

Geo-Shapes

Make shapes that have:

Shapes may vary.

| 3 sides | 4 sides | 5 sides |

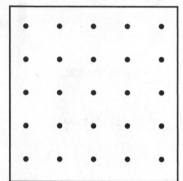 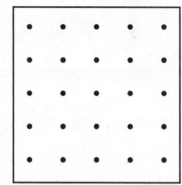 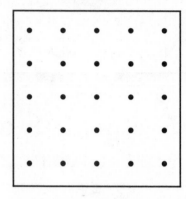

How many corners?   How many corners?   How many corners?

_____   _____   _____

Make shapes that have:

| 6 corners | 7 corners | 8 corners |

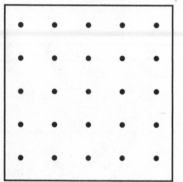 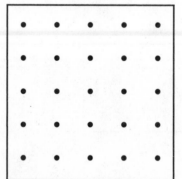 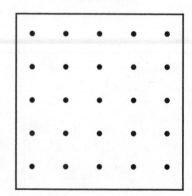

How many sides?   How many sides?   How many sides?

_____   _____   _____

Is there a pattern in the number of sides and corners?
What is the pattern?

_____

Name _____

Guess the Shape

Look at the number pattern.
Imagine you have connected the numbers.
Ring the shape you think you would make.
Then connect the numbers to check.

1. 1-4-7-8-5-2-1

↓ 1   2   3
  •   •   •
  4   5   6
  •   •   •
  7   8   9
  •   •   •

triangle   rectangle   square

2. 3-6-9-8-7-5-3

1   2   3 ↓
•   •   •
4   5   6
•   •   •
7   8   9
•   •   •

triangle   rectangle   square

3. 6-7-8-9-14-19-24-
18-12-6

1   2   3   4   5
•   •   •   •   •
6   7   8   9   10
•   •   •   •   •
11   12   13   14   15
•   •   •   •   •
16   17   18   19   20
•   •   •   •   •
21   22   23   24   25
•   •   •   •   •

triangle   rectangle   square

4. 3-7-11-17-23-19-
15-9-3

1   2   3   4   5
•   •   •   •   •
6   7   8   9   10
•   •   •   •   •
11   12   13   14   15
•   •   •   •   •
16   17   18   19   20
•   •   •   •   •
21   22   23   24   25
•   •   •   •   •

triangle   rectangle   square

Name _____

Symmetry Squares

Work with a partner. Use different colored crayons.
Color some squares on one side of the line.
Your partner colors the other half to match the squares
you colored. Color one row at a time. Take turns going first.

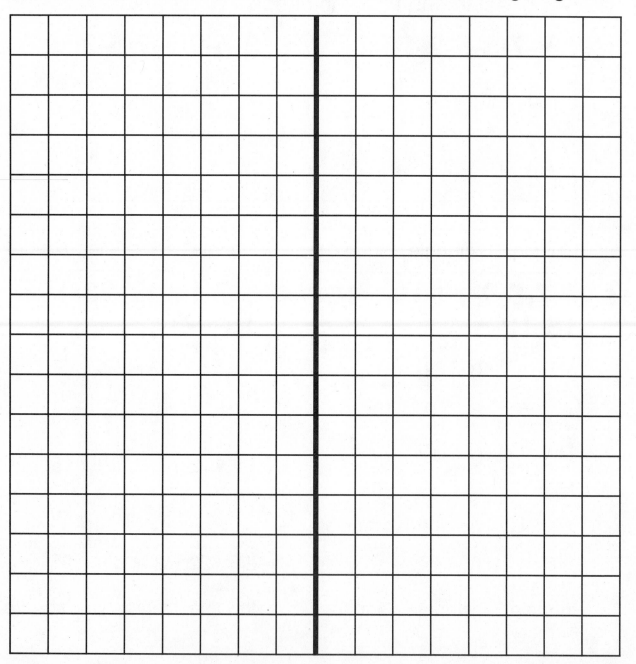

Use with text pages 259–260.

Puzzle Pieces

Write the letter of each piece on the puzzle piece below that is congruent.

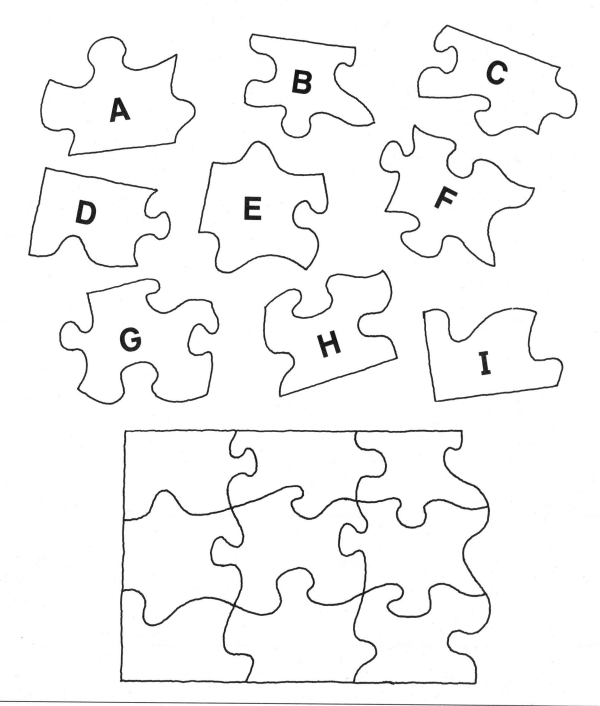

Name _____

Hidden Counters

Play with a partner. Stand a book between you to keep your game boards hidden. Each player places 3 counters on points on the board. Then take turns guessing where your partner has placed them. Make a guess like this: *Is it at A,3?* Mark an X on the point for each wrong guess.
Play until one of you finds all 3 counters.

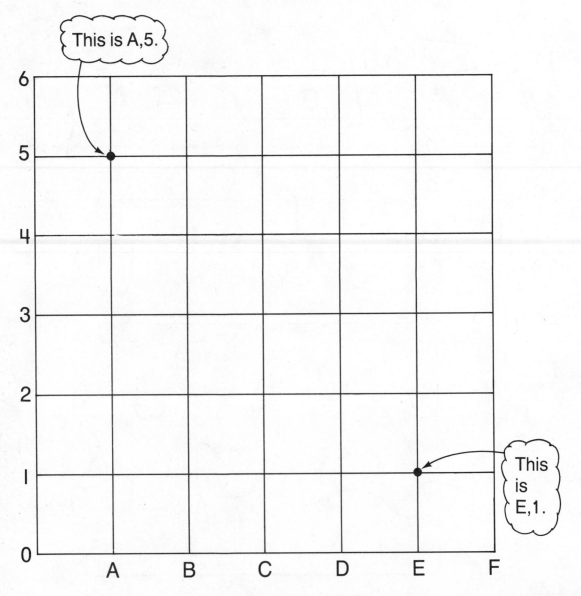

Use with text page 263.

Count Back Bingo

You need: a spinner with these numbers:
a set of number cards 1 to 5
20 counters

Rules: Put the number cards facedown in a pile.
Spin the spinner and pick a number card.
Count back to subtract the number on the card from the number on the spinner.
Find the answer on the game board and cover it with a counter.
Play until you have 5 counters in a row.
Play 3 games.

Spinner numbers: 33, 50, 28, 16, 45

Cards: 1, 2, 3, 4, 5

15	31	43	29	12
27	42	14	26	40
47	30	41	48	28
44	46	45	13	25
11	23	49	24	32

Name _____

Bowling for Tens

Dear Family,
   Your child has just completed a lesson on subtracting tens. To play this game you will need a number cube marked in tens — 10 – 60 — or small cards marked 10 – 60.

Take turns.

The first player rolls the number cube or draws a card.

Read the number on the top of the cube or on the card.

Cross out one pin to subtract each ten.

For example, if you roll a 30, cross out 3 pins.

If the number on the cube is more than the number of pins you have left, you lose your turn.

The first player to cross out all the pins wins.

Player 1	Player 2

Tens Checkers

Rules: 1. Each player puts 6 counters on the 6 white squares nearest the top or bottom edge of the checkerboard.

2. Take turns. Move 1 counter to a subtraction square. Solve the exercise aloud.

3. If your answer is right, stay on the square. If your answer is wrong, move back to the white square.

4. Move your counters to the opposite side of the board by moving from one subtraction square to the next.

5. The first player to reach the opposite side with all 6 counters wins.

	14-10		65-20		42-30
26-10		24-20		79-40	
	56-30		36-20		17-10
67-20		94-10		49-30	
	81-30		33-20		62-10
54-10		73-30		87-80	

Name _____

Color the Squares

Color the squares on each grid. Write a subtraction sentence that tells how many squares are colored. Then write a sentence that tells how many are <u>not</u> colored.

Use the 50-block grid.

1. Color 20 squares.

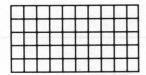

$$50 - 30 = 20$$

_____

2. Color 17 squares.

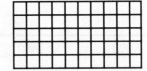

_____

_____

Use the 100-block grid.

3. Color 25 squares.

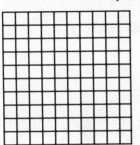

_____

_____

4. Color 40 squares.

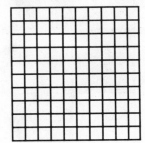

_____

_____

Name Change

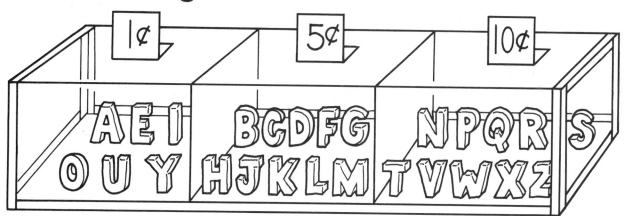

1. Buy the letters in your first name.

   How much does your name cost? _____
   Start with $1 ○ $1 . Ring the best
   estimate for your change.

   more than 50¢   less than 50¢

Work Space

2. Buy the letters in a friend's first name.

   How much does the name cost? _____
   Start with $1 ○ $1 . Ring the best
   estimate for your change.

   more than 50¢   less than 50¢

3. Buy the letters in a relative's first name.

   How much does the name cost? _____
   Start with $1 ○ $1 . Ring the best
   estimate for your change.

   more than 50¢   less than 50¢

Name _____

What Did they Buy?

Use punchout dimes and pennies to subtract.
Draw lines to show what each one bought.

1. Juan had 25¢.
Now he has 7¢.
What did he buy?

2. Karen had 38¢.
She has 22¢ left.
What did she buy?

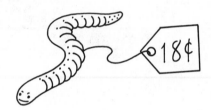

3. Nick had 30¢.
He got 17¢ change.
What did he buy?

4. Julie had 26¢.
She has 9¢ left.
What did she buy?

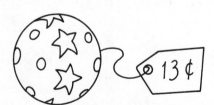

Name _____

Scavenger Hunt

Dear Family,
    Your child is learning to solve word problems by finding missing data. Help your child use the missing data to write subtraction sentences.

1. **Living room:** Count the number of chairs. Count the number of tables. We have ____ chairs and ____ tables. How many more chairs than tables does your family have?

    ____ ◯ ____ ☐ ____

2. **Bathroom:** Count the number of towels. Count the number of facecloths. We have ____ towels and ____ facecloths. How many more towels than facecloths does your family have?

    ____ ◯ ____ ☐ ____

3. **Bedroom:** Count the number of pillows. Count the number of blankets. We have ____ pillows and ____ blankets. How many more pillows than blankets does your family have?

    ____ ◯ ____ ☐ ____

Tens and Ones Bingo

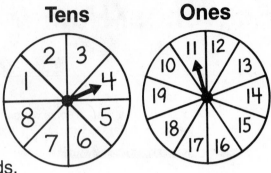

Tens   **Ones**

You need: a friend, 2 spinners like these:

40 counters, and 2 game boards.

Rules: Take turns. Spin both spinners.
Read the number like this: _____ tens and _____ ones.
If a number on your game board can be traded to make
the spinner number, put a counter on the number.
For example, 2 <u>tens</u> and 12 <u>ones</u> = 32.

spinner
numbers

game board
numbers

The first player to cover 5 numbers in a row wins.

22	65	38	80	35
51	34	26	91	83
98	62	40	87	71
47	69	94	56	29
78	75	53	44	67

Name _____

Making Change

Dear Family,
   Your child has just learned about subtracting 2-digit numbers using models. Have
your child show 99¢ in dimes and pennies. Provide newspaper ads for grocery items and
have your child pick something to buy and subtract to find the change.

Pick something to buy that costs less than 99¢.
Take away pennies and dimes to subtract the cost.
Trade 1 dime for 10 pennies when you need to.
Write how much money is left.

1.

Dimes	Pennies
☐	☐
9	9
–	
—	—

_____ ¢

2.

Dimes	Pennies
☐	☐
9	9
–	
—	—

_____ ¢

3.

Dimes	Pennies
☐	☐
9	9
–	
—	—

_____ ¢

4.

Dimes	Pennies
☐	☐
9	9
–	
—	—

_____ ¢

Name _____

Match the Picture

Write a subtraction exercise to match the picture.
Write the numbers to show the trade if there is one.

1.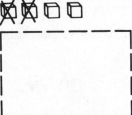

Tens	Ones

$-$
_____

2.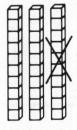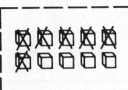

Tens	Ones

$-$
_____

3.

Tens	Ones

$-$
_____

4.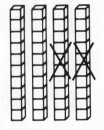

Tens	Ones

$-$
_____

What Is Missing?

Find the missing numbers.
See how fast you can reach the end of each path.

1. $47 - \underline{} = 33$

$$- \,\overline{}$$

$$20 - \underline{} = 12$$

$$- \,\overline{}$$

2. $94 - \underline{} = 80$ $\qquad 6 - \underline{} = 0$

$$- \,\overline{}$$

$$50 - \underline{} = 38$$

$$- \,\overline{}$$

3. $64 - \underline{} = 61$ $\qquad 20 - \underline{} = 0$

$$- \,\overline{}$$

$$21 - \underline{} = 10$$

$$- \,\overline{}$$

4. Make up your own. $\qquad 3 - \underline{} = 0$

$$\underline{} - \underline{} = \underline{}$$

$$- \,\overline{}$$

$$\underline{} - \underline{} = \underline{}$$

$$- \,\overline{}$$

$$\underline{} - \underline{} = \underline{0}$$

Make a Problem

Choose a number to go in the box.

1.

$$\begin{array}{r} 2\ 5 \\ -\ \boxed{4} \\ \hline \end{array}$$
more than 20

$$\begin{array}{r} 2\ 5 \\ -\ \boxed{7} \\ \hline \end{array}$$
less than 20

$$\begin{array}{r} 2\ 5 \\ -\ \boxed{} \\ \hline \end{array}$$
more than 20

$$\begin{array}{r} 2\ 5 \\ -\ \boxed{} \\ \hline \end{array}$$
less than 20

2.

$$\begin{array}{r} 3\ 3 \\ -\ \boxed{} \\ \hline \end{array}$$
less than 30

$$\begin{array}{r} 3\ 3 \\ -\ \boxed{} \\ \hline \end{array}$$
more than 30

$$\begin{array}{r} 3\ 3 \\ -\ \boxed{} \\ \hline \end{array}$$
less than 30

$$\begin{array}{r} 3\ 3 \\ -\ \boxed{} \\ \hline \end{array}$$
more than 30

3.

$$\begin{array}{r} 4\ 6 \\ -\ \boxed{} \\ \hline \end{array}$$
more than 40

$$\begin{array}{r} 4\ 6 \\ -\ \boxed{} \\ \hline \end{array}$$
less than 40

$$\begin{array}{r} 4\ 6 \\ -\ \boxed{} \\ \hline \end{array}$$
more than 40

$$\begin{array}{r} 4\ 6 \\ -\ \boxed{} \\ \hline \end{array}$$
less than 40

Name _____

Check It Out!

Work with a friend.
Your friend chooses a number.
You subtract, then add as shown below to get the
same number.   Take turns.

1. Choose a number greater than 50. _____

 Subtract 20. _____

 Add 10.   _____

 Add 10.   _____

> Are these numbers
> the same?

2. Choose a number greater than 30. _____

 Subtract 10. _____

 Add 5.   _____

 Add 5.   _____

3. Choose a number greater than 40. _____

 Subtract 18. _____

 Add 6.   _____

 Add 6.   _____

 Add 6.   _____

4. Make up your own with your friend.

Name _____

Shape Race

You need a friend, 2 , and 2 number cubes labeled 1 to 6.

Take turns. Roll the 2 number cubes twice.
Write two 2-digit numbers. Subtract the smaller from the greater number.
If the difference is between 0 – 20, write the subtraction sentence

in the ◯ .

If the difference is between 21 – 30, write the subtraction sentence

in the △ .

If the difference is between 31 – 55, write the subtraction sentence

in the ▢ .

The first player to fill all 3 shapes wins.

Hint: Decide which shape you want to fill, then think about what

the difference should be. Use your to check.

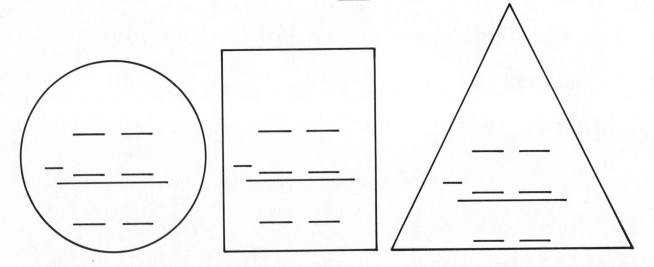

Name _____

That's Odd!

Here are some rules about odd and even numbers.
Use your calculator and check to see if they are true.
Record 2 problems for each rule.

1. Pick any two odd numbers.
Add them.   _____

The answer will be an even number.   _____

2. Subtract any odd number from
any other odd number.   _____

The answer will be an even number.   _____

3. Subtract any even number from
any odd number.   _____

The answer will be an odd number.   _____

Think of the rules. Ring the answers. Check with your calculator.

4. Which two numbers have
a sum of 78?   **62**   **24**   **56**

5. Which two numbers have
a difference of 33?   **19**   **62   23**

6. Which two numbers have
a difference of 48?   **88   96**   **44**

Name _____

Spin to Win

| S T A R T | 60 −20 | 44 −30 | 131 −68 | Go back 1 space. | 57 −28 | 80 −30 | 113 −76 | Spin again. |

| FINISH 77 −50 | | | | | | | 126 −89 |

You need: 1 or more friends, 1 spinner, 1 marker

for each player, paper and pencil, and a [calculator].

| | 50 −40 |

| Go back 2 spaces. | | 72 −54 |

| 26 −17 | Rules: Put your marker on START. Spin the spinner. Move that number of spaces. Decide if the exercise on the space can be solved using mental math, | Lose 1 turn. |

| 164 −99 | paper and pencil, or a [calculator]. | 97 −60 |

| 60 −30 | Solve it. All players need to agree that the answer is right. Take turns. The first person to get to FINISH wins. | 83 −45 |

| Lose 1 turn. | | Go back to start. |

| 153 −65 | 88 −70 | 20 −20 | 44 −27 | Spin again. | 178 −87 | 91 −66 | 146 −97 |

Name _____

Crossnumber Puzzle

Solve the puzzle.

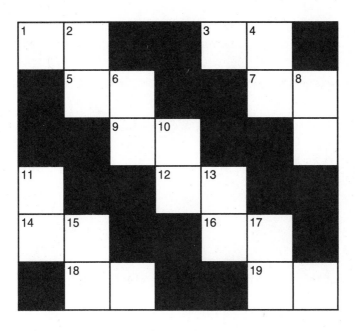

Across

1. 61 − 38
3. 7 + 7 + 7
5. 6 ones, 4 tens
7. 82 − 48
9. 60, 59, 58, ☐
12. 50 − 19
14. 27 + 36
16. 70 − 7
18. 5 tens
19. 3, 6, 9, ☐

Down

2. 93 − 59
4. 4 + 3 + 4 + 2
6. 70 − 5
8. 10, 20, 30, ☐
10. 58 + 15
11. 4 less than 60
13. 7 more than 9
15. 64 − 29
17. 34, 33, 32, ☐

Name _____

Estimate and Measure

1. About how much taller is your  than your ?

Estimate: _____   Measurement: _____

2. About how many inches is it from the floor to

the top of the 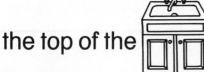?

Estimate: _____   Measurement: _____

3. About how far is it between the  and

the ?

Estimate: _____   Measurement: _____

4. About how far is it between the  and

the ?

Estimate: _____   Measurement: _____

Dividing Lines

Draw lines to show equal parts.

1. halves

2. thirds

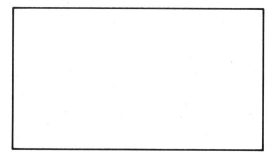

3. fourths

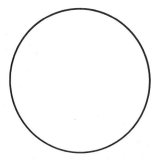

4. halves

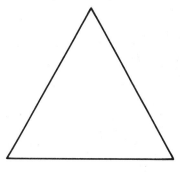

5. Show different ways to make fourths.

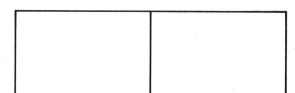

Folding Fractions

Follow the directions.

1. Fold a piece of paper once.
Unfold it.
How many parts do you see? _____

Color the paper to show $\frac{1}{2}$
of the equal parts.

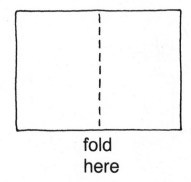

fold
here

---

2. Fold a piece of paper twice
as shown. Unfold it.
How many parts do you see? _____

Color the paper to show $\frac{3}{4}$
of the equal parts.

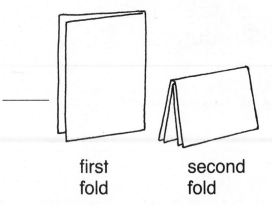

first   second
fold   fold

---

3. Fold a piece of paper three
times as shown. Unfold it.
How many parts do you see? _____

Color the paper to show $\frac{1}{8}$
of the equal parts.

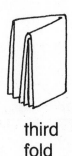

third
fold

Name _____

Follow the Fractions

- Look at each fraction picture as you move down the river.
- Choose the fraction that matches the picture.
- Draw a line to the dot next to the matching fraction.

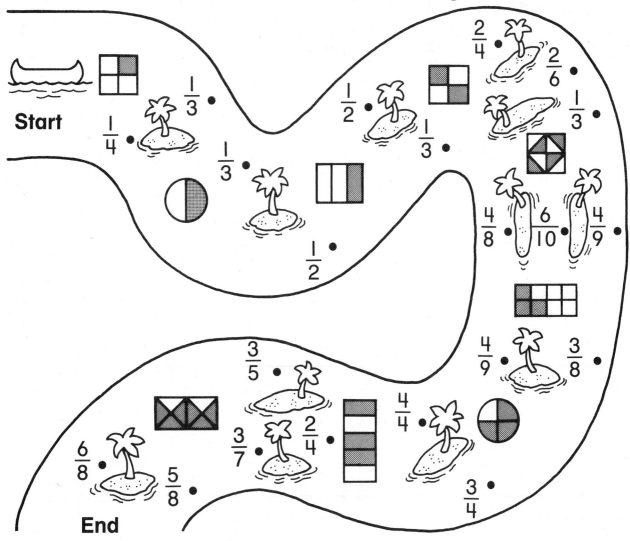

Name _____

Fraction Fun

Play with a partner or in a group. Use a paper clip and
a pencil to make the spinner.
Each player gets 8 red counters and 8 yellow counters.
Each puts a marker on the **Start** box.
Take turns. Spin and move your marker that many spaces.
Show the fraction on the space with counters.

For example, to show $\frac{1}{5}$:

Tell whether the fraction is for the red part or the
yellow part.

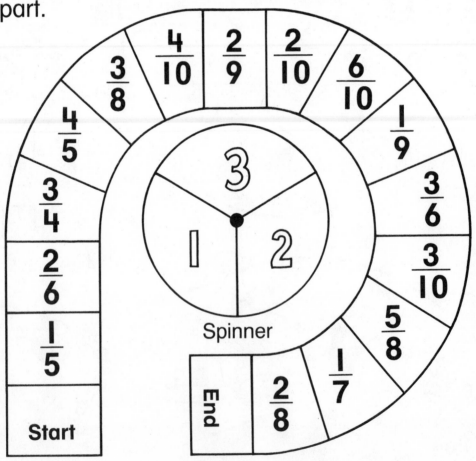

Spinner

Name _____

Fraction Math

Estimate without counting which 2 figures in each row show
the same fraction for the shaded part.
Ring those figures.
Then count and write the fractions to check.

1.

 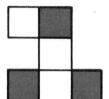 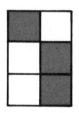 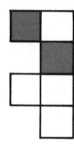

—— shaded   —— shaded   —— shaded   —— shaded

2.

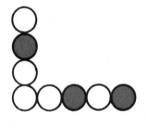  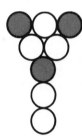

—— shaded   —— shaded   —— shaded   —— shaded

3.

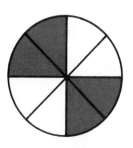 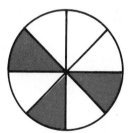 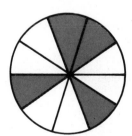

—— shaded   —— shaded   —— shaded   —— shaded

Name _____

Coloring Fractions

Color to show the fractions.

1. $\frac{1}{3}$ yellow

$\frac{1}{3}$ blue

$\frac{1}{3}$ orange

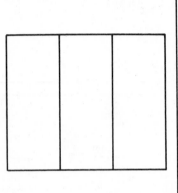

2. $\frac{1}{5}$ red

$\frac{2}{5}$ yellow

$\frac{2}{5}$ blue

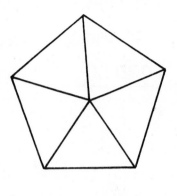

3. $\frac{3}{8}$ red

$\frac{1}{8}$ purple

$\frac{4}{8}$ orange

4. $\frac{2}{6}$ purple

$\frac{2}{6}$ yellow

$\frac{2}{6}$ red

5. Make up your own.
Use three different colors to color the boxes.
Write the fractions.

_____   _____   _____

Size Them Up

Write > (greater than), < (less than), or = (the same)
in each ○. Use your fraction pieces to help.

1. $\dfrac{1}{2}$ ○ $\dfrac{1}{4}$

2. $\dfrac{2}{4}$ ○ $\dfrac{4}{8}$

3. $\dfrac{1}{3}$ ○ $\dfrac{1}{2}$

4. $\dfrac{2}{8}$ ○ $\dfrac{1}{4}$

5. $\dfrac{3}{8}$ ○ $\dfrac{1}{4}$

6. $\dfrac{2}{3}$ ○ $\dfrac{5}{6}$

7. $\dfrac{3}{6}$ ○ $\dfrac{1}{2}$

8. $\dfrac{1}{4}$ ○ $\dfrac{1}{6}$

9. $\dfrac{3}{4}$ ○ $\dfrac{7}{8}$

10. $\dfrac{1}{3}$ ○ $\dfrac{2}{6}$

11. $\dfrac{2}{3}$ ○ $\dfrac{4}{6}$

12. $\dfrac{1}{2}$ ○ $\dfrac{5}{8}$

Name _____

Dot Count

Play with a partner.
Each of you needs a game sheet.
Roll a number cube marked 1 – 6.
Draw that many circles on your
scorecard. Roll again. Draw
that many dots in each circle.

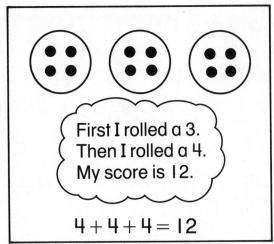

First I rolled a 3.
Then I rolled a 4.
My score is 12.

$4 + 4 + 4 = 12$

Skip count or write an addition sentence to find the total.
Take turns. The player with the highest score wins
the round.

Round 1

Round 2

Round 3

Round 4

Name _____

Skip Counting

Use your .

Press the keys in order. Write the numbers you see.

1. Skip count by 2s from 0 to 10.

ON/C	0	+	2	=	=	=	=	=

                2   4   6   8   10

How many times did you press $=$? 5

Finish the multiplication sentence: $2 \times 5 = 10$

2. Skip count by 3s from 0 to 12.

ON/C	0	+	3	=	=	=	=

      ___   ___   ___   ___

How many times did you press $=$? ____

Finish the multiplication sentence. ____ $\times$ ____ $=$ ____

3. Skip count by fours from 0 to 16.

ON/C	0	+	4	=	=	=	=

      ___   ___   ___   ___

Finish the multiplication sentence. ____ $\times$ ____ $=$ ____

Name _____

Give and Take

You need: I or more friends, play money, I number cube, and markers.

Rules: Take turns. Put the markers on START.
Ask I person to be the Banker.
Roll the number cube and move that many spaces.
Follow the directions on the space.

> **Take:** You get money from the Banker.
> **Give:** You give money to the Banker.

If you land on $, you get $5 from the Banker.
If you do not have enough money to give the Banker,
go back to START.
The player with the most money at FINISH wins.

S T A R T	Take 5 × $1.	Take 2 × $2.	Take 4 × $1.	Take 3 × $1 and go again.	$	Go back 3 spaces.	Lose I turn.

Take 4 × $3. Give 2 × $4.	$	Go back to start.	Give 3 × $4.	Give I × $3.	Take 3 × $2.	Give I × $2.

Go again.	Take I × $1.	Give 2 × $5.	Give 3 × $2.	$	Give 3 × $3.	Give 3 × $2. Take 3 × $3.	F I N I S H

Name _____

Turnarounds

Match the turnarounds.

Use your to check.

1. **4** × **3** = ☐   **A** **2** × **5** = ☐

2. **5** × **3** = ☐   **B** **3** × **5** = ☐

3. **2** × **3** = ☐   **C** **3** × **4** = ☐

4.  **5** × **2** = ☐   **D** **3** × **2** = ☐

5. **1** × **3** = ☐   **E** **2** × **4** = ☐

6. **4** × **2** = ☐   **F** **3** × **1** = ☐

Name _____

Money Riddles

Solve each riddle.

Write the money amounts on the coins or bills.

1. I have 46¢.
Two coins
are dimes.

2. I have 62¢.
One coin is a
half dollar.

3. I have $1.36.

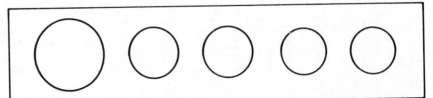

4. I have $2.00.

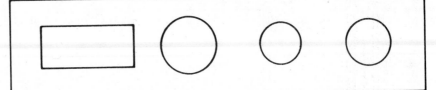

5. I have $1.25.
I do not have
any quarters.

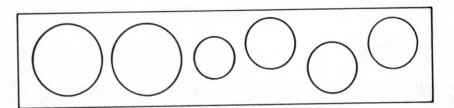

The Elephant Family

Read the story.
Decide what numbers to
write in the spaces.
Write the numbers and finish
the picture. Use only even
numbers. Write a division
sentence to describe the story.
Then finish writing the story.

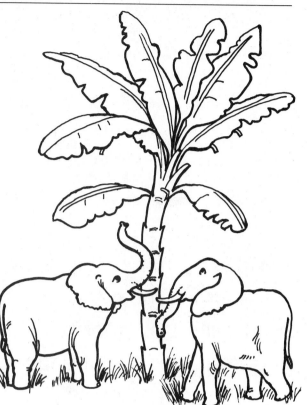

Edna and Edward Elephant live in Africa. One day, the

____ elephants went for a walk. It was lunchtime.
"Look, Edna!" cried Edward. "Bananas!"
Edna looked up. She saw a tall banana tree with

____ bunches of ripe bananas. The ____ elephants shook
the tree. One big bunch of bananas fell to the ground.

Edward counted ____ bananas. Edna and Edward shared

the bananas. They each ate ____ bananas for lunch.

After lunch, the elephants _____

_____.

Division sentence: _____

Name _____

Make It Equal

Dear Family,
   Your child is learning about division by separating things into equal groups. For this game you will need 20 paper clips or other small objects, and slips of paper with the numbers 1, 2, 4, 5, and 10 written on them, one number to a card.

Mix up the number cards and put them in a pile.
Take turns. The first player picks a number card and separates the paper clips into that many equal groups. Together, decide if the task of dividing the paper clips was done correctly. Write the division sentence on the score pad. Put the number card on the bottom of the pile. Each player gets 3 turns.
To find the winner, add the 3 scores.

_____'s Score Pad
(Name)

____ ÷ ____ = ____

____ ÷ ____ = ____

____ ÷ ____ = ____

Total ____

_____'s Score Pad
(Name)

____ ÷ ____ = ____

____ ÷ ____ = ____

____ ÷ ____ = ____

Total ____

Addison-Wesley | All Rights Reserved

142   Use with text pages 343–344.   **CS-2**

Name _____

Dear Family,
    Our class is learning to multiply and divide. This game will help your child understand the relationship between multiplication and division.

Write the numbers 1, 2, or 3 inside a circle on each of 6 cards. Write 2, 3, or 4 inside a square on 6 more cards.
Place the cards facedown in 2 piles.
Take turns. Draw 1 card from each pile.
Write the number on the circle card in the circle below.
Write the number on the square card in the square.
Write the answer in the triangle.
The answer in the triangle is the score.
Write the related division sentence below that.
Each player takes 3 turns. Add up the scores in the triangles.
The player with the highest score wins.

1. ◯ × ☐ = △
score

△ ÷ ◯ = ☐

1. ◯ × ☐ = △
score

△ ÷ ◯ = ☐

2. ◯ × ☐ = △
score

△ ÷ ◯ = ☐

2. ◯ × ☐ = △
score

△ ÷ ◯ = ☐

3. ◯ × ☐ = △
score

△ ÷ ◯ = ☐

3. ◯ × ☐ = △
score

△ ÷ ◯ = ☐

Total = _____

Total = _____

Problem Solving

Name _____

Spend It on Stamps

Write a multiplication or a division sentence to solve.

1. Jiro wants to buy 3 baseball stamps. What is the total cost?

_____

2. Gwen has 15¢. How many heart stamps can she buy?

_____

3. Max has 20¢. How many flag stamps can he buy?

_____

4. How much does Paola need to buy 5 flower stamps?

_____

5. Megan has 10¢. Can she buy 3 baseball stamps?

_____

6. Valerie has 18¢. How many baseball stamps can she buy?

_____

7. Sam wants to buy 5 flag stamps. How much does he need?

_____

8. Ted spent 14¢ on flower stamps. How many did he get?

_____

Addison-Wesley | All Rights Reserved

144 Use with text page 348. **CS-2**

What Does It Mean?

Tell what the black digit means.
Ring the answer.

Hundreds	Tens	Ones
1	2	3

→ | 123 |

1.   I hundred   I ten   I one

2.  8 hundreds   8 tens   8 ones

3.  4 hundreds   4 tens   4 ones

4.  6 hundreds   6 tens   6 ones

5.   3 hundreds   3 tens   3 ones

6.  2 hundreds   2 tens   2 ones

Name _____

Building Blocks

Use your base-ten blocks.
Estimate how many hundreds, tens, and ones will cover the book.
Then cover each book and count.

1. 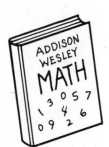 Your math book

Estimate ____

Hundreds	Tens	Ones

Hundreds	Tens	Ones

Count ____

2.  Your reading book

Estimate ____

Hundreds	Tens	Ones

Hundreds	Tens	Ones

Count ____

3.  Your favorite book

Estimate ____

Hundreds	Tens	Ones

Hundreds	Tens	Ones

Count ____

Flip It!

Play with a partner.

Flip 6 counters onto the board.

Record your score. Take turns.

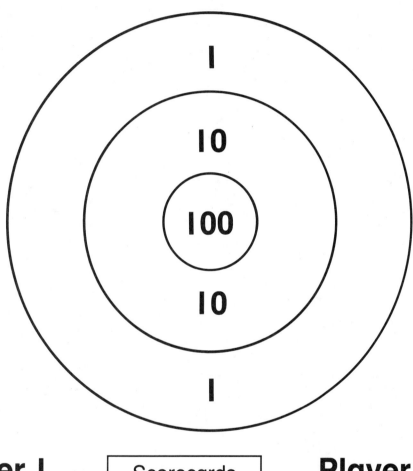

Player I   Scorecards   **Player 2**

_____   _____

_____   _____

_____   _____

_____   _____

Number Paths

Complete the path by writing numbers
in each shape as you go. Use the code.

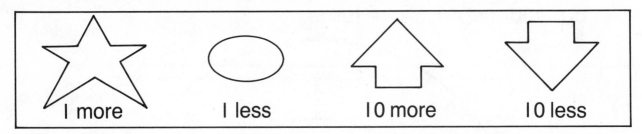

| I more | I less | 10 more | 10 less |

Start 553

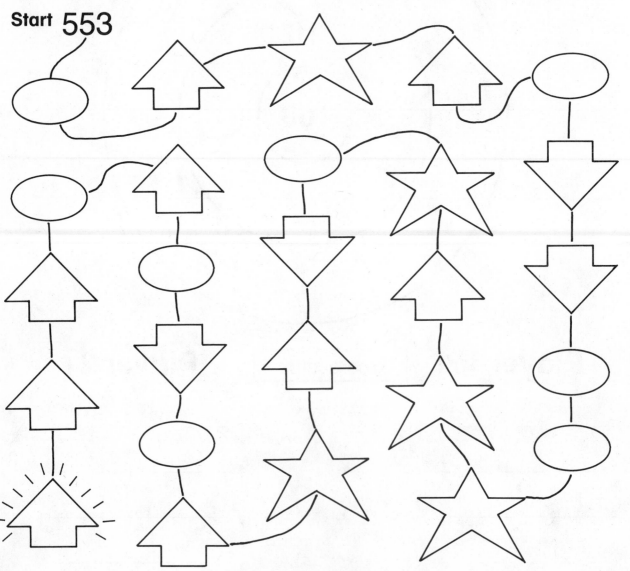

Use with text pages 359 – 360.

Name _____

Before, After, Between

Dear Family,
    Your child is learning about 3-digit numbers. Play this game to review numbers before, after, and between.

Make cards for each of these numbers:

    355 through 375.

Shuffle and deal the cards.

The player with card 365 goes first.

362
363
364
365
368
369
370

Player 3
I place a card before, after, or between the other numbers

Player 1
I go first because I have 365.

Player 2
I place a card before or after 365.

Play continues around the table until all cards are played.

Name _____

Play Time

Decide which operation you will use.
Choose a calculation method and solve.
Write the answer in a sentence.

1. The Hawks scored 32 points in the first half of the basketball game. They scored 28 points in the second half. What was the total score?

_____

- -

_____

2. 80 students signed up for soccer. 50 students signed up for softball. How many more students will play soccer?

_____

- -

_____

3. 20 children ran in relay races. There were 4 teams. How many children were on each team?

_____

- -

_____

4. 240 fans watched the game. The gym has 300 seats in all. How many seats were empty?

_____

- -

_____

Graph-a-Game

Play this game with a friend.
Make two cards for each number.

| 0 | | 2 | | 4 | | 6 | | 8 | |
| | 1 | | 3 | | 5 | | 7 | | 9 |

Here is how you play:

1. Put all the cards into a bag.
2. Each player picks 3 numbers and makes the greatest 3-digit number he or she can.
3. Compare numbers.
4. The player with the greater number colors a box in the graph.
5. Play until one player colors all the boxes.

Player 1	Player 2

Name _____

Less Is Best

Color the fewest bills and coins you can use
to buy each item.

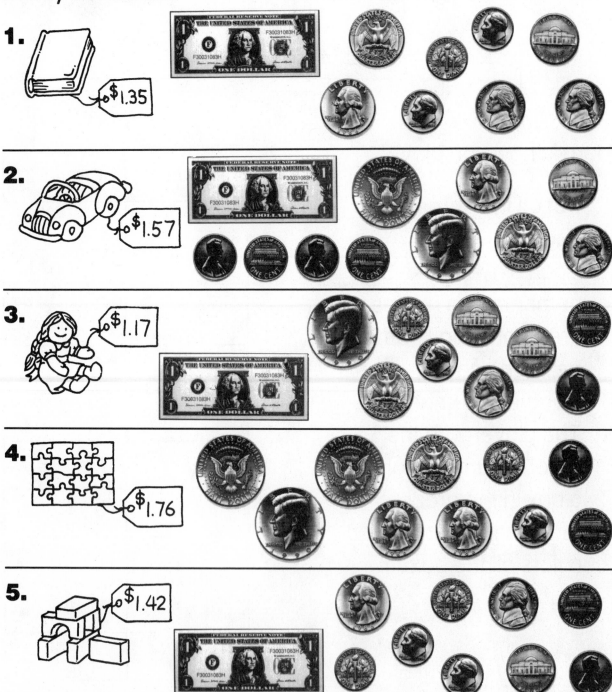

1. $1.35

2. $1.57

3. $1.17

4. $1.76

5. $1.42

Use with text pages 367–368.

Name _____

Choose Your Own

Choose one of the titles.

Write an addition story or a subtraction story.

Use 2-digit numbers.

Write question and answer sentences. Share your story.

A Sticker Story	**A Bus Trip Story**
A Picnic	**A Zoo Story**

Find the Addends

Use the numbers in the box.
Write the addends that make each sum.

Clues: 1. Add the ones.
          2. See if there is a
             trade.

106	122
27	133
	219

1.

```
    [ ]            [1]            [1]
  1 0 6          ____           ____
+ ____         + ____         + ____
  2 3 9          1 6 0          3 4 1
```

2.

```
   [1]            [ ]            [ ]
  ____           ____           ____
+ ____         + ____         + ____
  1 3 3          2 5 5          2 2 8
```

3.

```
   [1]            [1]            [1]
  ____           ____           ____
+ ____         + ____         + ____
  3 2 5          2 4 6          3 5 2
```

Use with text pages 375 – 376.

Name _____

Initial Scores

An initial is the first letter of a word.

Write your first and last name initials. ____ ____

Ring the number that goes with each of your initials.

A	B	C	D	E	F	G	H	I	J	K	L	M	N
30	40	50	60	70	80	90	30	40	50	60	70	80	90

O	P	Q	R	S	T	U	V	W	X	Y	Z
30	40	50	60	70	80	90	30	40	50	60	70

Add to find your score. ____ + ____ = ____

Pick 5 friends.

Write their first names on the chart.

Write their first and last name initials.

Find the points for each letter.

Add the points to find the score.

Name	Initials	Points	Score
1. _____	____ ____	____ ____	___ + ___ = ___
2. _____	____ ____	____ ____	___ + ___ = ___
3. _____	____ ____	____ ____	___ + ___ = ___
4. _____	____ ____	____ ____	___ + ___ = ___
5. _____	____ ____	____ ____	___ + ___ = ___

Name _____

Treasure Hunt

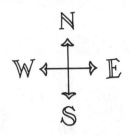

Look at the treasure map.
Finish each set of directions.

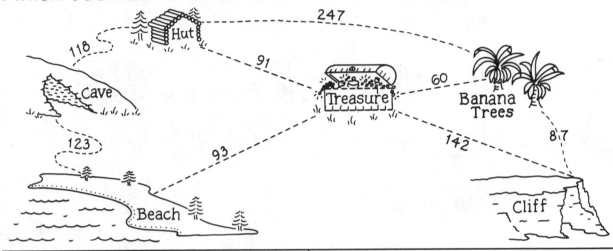

Walk 307 steps to find the treasure. Start at the hut. Walk 247 steps to the _____ . Go ____ steps to the treasure.	Walk 229 steps to find the treasure. Start at the banana trees. Walk ____ steps to the cliff. Go ____ steps to the treasure.
Walk 216 steps to find the treasure. Start at the cave. Walk 123 steps to the _____ . Go ____ steps to the treasure.	Walk 209 steps to find the treasure. Start at the cave. Walk ____ steps to the hut. Go ____ steps to the treasure.

Name _____

Puzzle Problems

Choose a calculation method and solve.
Write the answer in a sentence.

1. Denise just finished a jigsaw puzzle that had
300 pieces. She is starting a new puzzle that has
450 pieces. How many more pieces does the new
puzzle have?

_____

- -

_____

2. Lonny's model airplane has 95 pieces. So far he has
put together 46 pieces. How many pieces does he still
have to put together?

_____

- -

_____

3. Andrea has two dinosaur kits. The Stegosaurus has
42 pieces. The Tyrannosaurus has 68 pieces. How
many more pieces does the Tyrannosaurus have?

_____

- -

_____

4. Brian's father collects model boats. He has 137 sailboats
and 154 power boats. How many model boats does he
have altogether?

_____

- -

_____

Name _____

Dear Family,
    We are learning to subtract with trading 1 ten for 10 ones. Help your child practice.
You will need 12 slips of paper with the numbers below written on them.

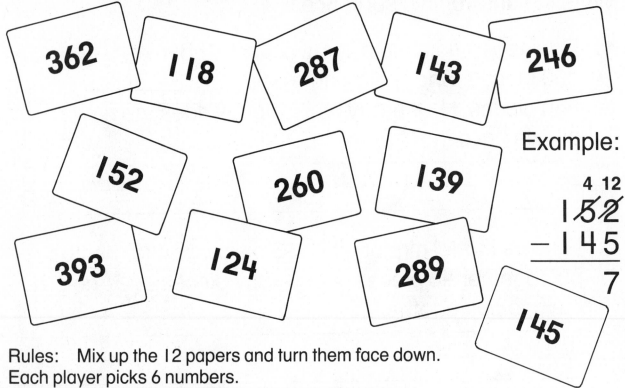

Example:

$$\begin{array}{r} \overset{4\ \ 12}{1\cancel{5}\cancel{2}} \\ -\ 1\ 4\ 5 \\ \hline 7 \end{array}$$

Rules: Mix up the 12 papers and turn them face down.
Each player picks 6 numbers.
Use the 6 numbers to make 3 subtraction problems.
Do your work in the space below.
Arrange the numbers so that you have to trade.
Subtract the smaller numbers from the larger ones.
If you did not trade, your score is 5 points for each.
If you traded 1 ten for 10 ones, your score is 10 points for each.

Name _____

Telephone Math

Dear Family,
    Your child is learning to trade 1 hundred for 10 tens to subtract. Use the numbers in your telephone number to help your child practice trading.

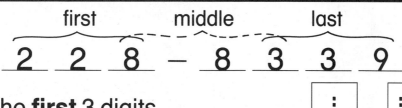

first   middle   last

2   2   8   –   8   3   3   9

1. Write the **first** 3 digits of this phone number. Trade I hundred for I0 tens.

2. Write the **middle** 3 digits of the phone number above. Trade I hundred for I0 tens.

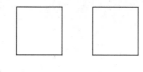

3. Write the **last** 3 digits of the phone number above. Trade I hundred for I0 tens.

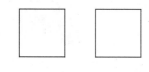

Write your telephone number.

_____ _____ _____ — _____ _____ _____ _____

Use your number and follow the steps above.

First 3 digits.   Middle 3 digits.   Last 3 digits.

Crossnumber Puzzle Fun

Solve the puzzle.

Across
1. 17 + 17
3. 862 − 134
5. 5 hundreds, 3 ones
7. 415 + 205
8. 560 − 534
12. 3 ones, 2 tens
14. 180 + 287
16. 771 − 129
18. 590 − 1
19. 77, 78, 79, ☐

Down
1. 20, 25, 30, ☐
2. 540 − 138
3. 27 + 45
4. the number after 199
6. 357, 358, 359, ☐
7. 59 + 1
9. 617 + 109
10. 385 − 137
11. 40 − 3
13. 4 tens, 8 ones, 3 hundreds
15. 70 − 1
17. 17, 18, 19, ☐

Name _____

To Market

You need: 2 players, markers, a number cube, punchout money, and
newspapers.

Rules: Find ads in the newspaper for the foods on the game board. Write
the prices of the foods on the spaces. Write other foods and their
prices on any blank spaces.

To start, each player gets $10 to spend. Estimate what you can
buy and make a shopping list.

Roll the cube and move that many spaces.

Buy the item on the space.

Use the punchout money to make change.

Play until your money is spent or you reach the exit. The player
who bought the most items on his or her list wins.

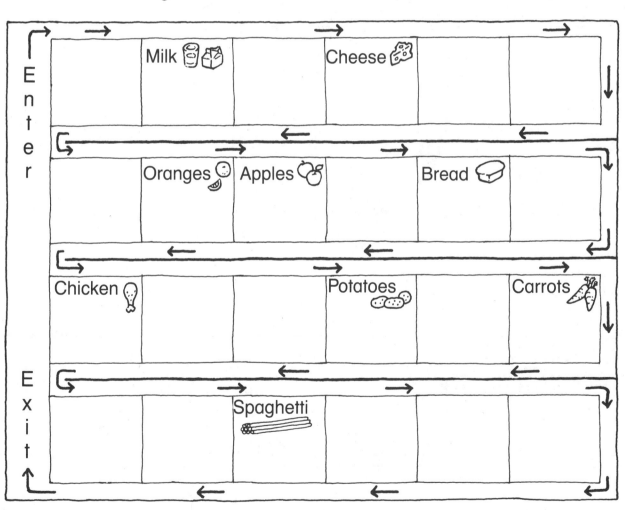

Name _____

At the Store

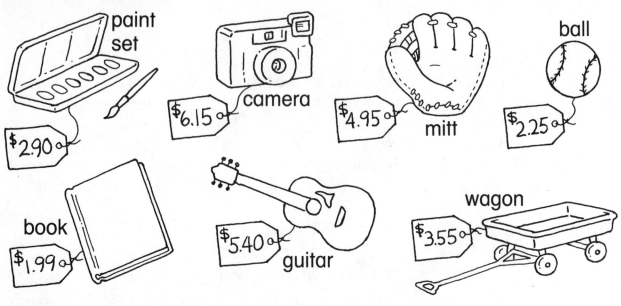

paint set $2.90
camera $6.15
mitt $4.95
ball $2.25
book $1.99
guitar $5.40
wagon $3.55

Solve.

1. Ramon had $7.50. He bought a paint set and a wagon. How much money does he have left?

   _____

2. Andy bought a mitt and 2 balls. How much did he spend?

   _____

3. Jenny had $3.50. She earned $2.75 more. How much will she have left after she buys the camera?

   _____

4. Luanna wants to buy a book and a guitar. She has $6.25 now. How much more does she need?

   _____